THE PUBLICATIONS COMMITEE OF THE COUNCIL

Twentyfifth annual report of the Council of Missions

Cooperating with the Church of Christ in Japan

THE PUBLICATIONS COMMITEE OF THE COUNCIL

Twentyfifth annual report of the Council of Missions
Cooperating with the Church of Christ in Japan

ISBN/EAN: 9783741169243

Manufactured in Europe, USA, Canada, Australia, Japa

Cover: Foto ©Andreas Hilbeck / pixelio.de

Manufactured and distributed by brebook publishing software (www.brebook.com)

THE PUBLICATIONS COMMITEE OF THE COUNCIL

Twentyfifth annual report of the Council of Missions

TWENTY-FIFTH ANNUAL REPORT OF THE COUNCIL OF MISSIONS

COÖPERATING WITH THE

CHURCH OF CHRIST IN JAPAN

ISSUED BY THE PUBLICATIONS COMMITTEE
OF THE COUNCIL

1902

Printed by THE FUKUIN PRINTING COMPANY,
Yokohama, Japan.

OFFICERS OF THE COUNCIL.

FOR 1902-1903

PRESIDENT . . . HENRY STOUT
VICE PRESIDENT . D. B. SCHNEDER
SECRETARY . . H. W. MYERS
TREASURER . . E. ROTHESAY MILLER

PUBLICATIONS COMMITTEE

WILLIAM IMBRIE
E. ROTHESAY MILLER
M. N. WYCKOFF
W. B. MCILWAINE
T. M. MACNAIR
A. D. HAIL
H. K. MILLER

SECRETARIES

OF THE

COÖPERATING MISSIONS

WILLIAM IMBRIE	TOKYO
HARVEY BROKAW	HIROSHIMA
M. N. WYCKOFF	TOKYO
HENRY STOUT	NAGASAKI
H. W. MYERS	TOKUSHIMA
C. NOSS	SENDAI
J. B. HAIL	WAKAYAMA
MISS CLARA D. LOOMIS	YOKOHAMA

CONTENTS

PROCEEDINGS OF THE COUNCIL . . 1

1 OPENING AND SESSIONS OF THE COUNCIL. . 1
2 REPORTS OF STANDING COMMITTEES . . . 2

    Publications and proposed review. . . . 2
    Sunday-school literature. 3
    Statistics 4
    Finances of the Council 4

3 REPORTS OF SPECIAL COMMITTEES APPOINTED BY THE LAST COUNCIL 4

    General report of the work of the year . . 4
    Ministerial relief 4
    Training of lay workers 5
    Distribution of forces. . . . 5

4 NEW BUSINESS 6

    Invitation to the Presbyterian Church of Canada 6
    Letter from Mrs. Martha Waddell . . . 6
    Minutes memorial of Mrs. Henry Stout and the Rev. Geo. C. Needham 6
    Letter of sympathy to Mr. Parrott . . . 7

Letter from Mr. Lawrence regarding the work of the Bible Societies Committee in Japan . . . .
Congratulatory minute to the Rev. James H. Ballagh . . . .
Action regarding the meetings of the Council and Conference . . . .
Printing of the proceedings of the Conference . . . .
Letter to the Synod . . . .
Committee of Arrangements for the next meeting of the Council . . . . . .
General report of the work of next year . .
Thanks of the Council to the President and also to the Karuizawa Church . . . .
Appointment of officers and committees . .
Close of the Council and next annual meeting . . . .

II GENERAL REPORT OF THE WORK OF THE YEAR. . . . .

INTRODUCTORY AND GENERAL . . . . .
EDUCATIONAL WORK . . . .
 Theo. Sch. 41; Bib. Wom. Sch. 44; Bib. Sch. for Evang. 46; Boys Sch. 46; Girls Sch. 49; Day Sch. 64; Kindergartens, 68; Industrial, 71; Night Cl. 72; Eng. Cl. 73; S. Sch. 74.
EVANGELISTIC WORK . . . .
 S. Jap. Miss. R.C.A. . . . . . .
 Miss. S. Presb. Ch. . . . .

Cumb. Presb. Miss.	87
W. Jap. Presb. Miss. (North).	90
N. Jap. Miss. R.C.A.	102
Miss. Ref. Ch. U.S.	107
E. Jap. Presb. Miss. (North).	112

III APPENDIX: 133
  1 WORK OF THE BIBLE SOCIETIES COMMITTEE
     IN JAPAN 133
  2 STATISTICAL TABLES 136
  3. FINANCIAL ITEMS OF THE DENDO KYOKU
     (BOARD OF HOME MISSIONS) OF THE
     CHURCH OF CHRIST IN JAPAN. 147
  4 PROCEEDINGS OF THE CONFERENCE . . . 148
  5 STATEMENT REGARDING PROPOSED REVIEW. 157

IV ROLL OF THE COUNCIL: 160
  EAST JAPAN MISSION OF THE PRESBYTERIAN
    CHURCH IN THE U. S. A. (NORTHERN) . 160
  WEST JAPAN MISSION OF THE PRESBYTERIAN
    CHURCH IN THE U. S. A. (NORTHERN). 161
  NORTH JAPAN MISSION OF THE REFORMED
    (Dutch) CHURCH IN AMERICA 162
  SOUTH JAPAN MISSION OF THE REFORMED
    (Dutch) CHURCH IN AMERICA 162
  MISSION OF THE PRESBYTERIAN CHURCH IN
    THE U. S. (SOUTHERN) 163
  MISSION OF THE REFORMED (GERMAN)
    CHURCH IN THE U. S. 164
  MISSION OF THE CUMBERLAND PRESBY-
    TERIAN CHURCH 164
  WOMANS UNION MISSIONARY SOCIETY . . 165

I
PROCEEDINGS
OF THE
TWENTY-FIFTH ANNUAL MEETING
OF THE COUNCIL

1 OPENING AND SESSIONS OF THE COUNCIL

The Council of Missions Coöperating with the Church of Christ in Japan assembled in the Union Church, Karuizawa, at 10 a.m., on July 30th, 1902. The President, the Rev. E. Rothesay Miller, preached the opening sermon, taking for his text, Mark 3 : 13-15.

The business session was opened at the call of the President. The Secretary of the Council being absent the Rev. H. B. Price was elected Secretary, and the Rev. W. E. Lampe Assistant Secretary. The roll-call showed thirty-seven members in attendance. All Presbyterian and Reformed missionaries in Karuizawa were invited to sit as corresponding members.

The Rev. D. C. Rankin, D.D. representing the Board of Foreign Missions of the Presbyterian Church in the U. S. (Southern), was welcomed by the President. In his response Dr. Rankin thanked the Council most cordially for postponing the time of its meeting in order that he might be present.

The morning sessions of the Council each day were preceded by a prayer-meeting from 9 till 9:30. On Sunday three services were held, two in English and one in Japanese.

2 REPORTS OF STANDING COMMITTEES

The following report of the Publications Committee* was adopted.

The twenty-fourth Annual Report of the Council was printed and distributed in the usual manner.

The following have been published by members of the Council:—As hitherto, *Yorokobi no Otozure* and *Chiisaki Otozure*, Mrs. E. R. Miller; *Yakō*, Mr. Jones; *Fukuin Geppō*, Mr. Brokaw, and *Tohoku Kyōkwai Jihō* by members of the Reformed (German) Mission. The following new works have been issued: An Easy Catechism, Mrs. Geo. P. Pierson and the Rev. M. Okuno. By Dr. Imbrie: A Door into Heaven, By the Old Well, A Birds-eye View of the Life of Christ, What think ye of Christ? and a second edition of The Gospel of God.

The question of publishing a review in connection with the Council was referred to a sub-committee, which has not yet rendered a report but suggests that the matter be further considered by the Council.

In accordance with the above suggestion, the question of publishing a review was carefully considered. A committee† was appointed to correspond with the missions composing the Council with the object o

---

* Messrs. Imbrie, E. Rothesay Miller, Wyckoff, McIlwaine MacNair, G. G. Hudson, H. K. Miller.
† Messrs. E. Rothesay Miller, S. P. Fulton, and Imbrie.

establishing such a review, and the Rev. E. Rothesay
Miller was appointed to represent the Council as editor.
The following report of the Committee on Sunday-
school Literature was adopted.

There has been no special change in the Sunday-school
publications, which still consist of the Teachers Monthly,
the Scholars Quarterly and the Primary Leaflet. These
have a circulation of about 600, 2000, and 6-7000,
respectively. The Teachers Monthly is edited by the Rev.
Messrs. F. Lombard and H. M. Landis; the Scholars
Quarterly by the Rev. Messrs. G. Draper and C.
Harrington; and the Primary Leaflet by Miss Cozad and
Miss Whitman.

The financial deficit has not been as yet materially
reduced, though there is a slight reduction accompanying
the increase in the number of subscriptions. The appor-
tionment of the deficit on the basis of all missionaries
(instead of on that of men only) has been accepted; but
has not yet been put into operation owing to a misunderstanding by the financial manager. This would slightly
inure to our benefit. The recommendation of the Council
of last year to adjust this deficit on the basis of the
church membership of the four churches was brought
before the Editorial Committee but was not adopted,
since on more careful examination it appeared that
it would afford but slight relief to the Council, would
benefit mainly the Baptists, and would weigh very
heavily upon the Congregationalists. In fact the stress
would have fallen exclusively upon them, and Dr. Greene
their business representative on the Editorial Committee
felt that the American Board Mission could hardly
assume the added burden.

The statistics of the year show a gain of over 30% on
the Sunday-school membership of the preceding year.
This is as it should be, seeing that the Sunday-school
membership is even yet far below the church member-

ship. The recommendations of the committee which appear in the Proceedings of last year are therefore still in place.*

The Committee on Statistics† presented its report which was adopted. A summary of it is presented in the tables printed in the Appendix.

The Financial Report for the year was referred to an Auditing Committee,‡ and on the report of the committee was adopted. The assessment for next year was fixed at six *yen* per member of the Council; and the President and Secretary of the Council were appointed a committee to furnish the Treasurer with the number of members in each mission properly liable to assessment for the year 1902-3.

3 REPORTS OF SPECIAL COMMITTEES APPOINTED BY THE LAST (OR A PRECEDING) COUNCIL

The General Report of the Work of the Year§ was read by the Rev. H. M. Landis. A resolution was adopted thanking Mr. Landis and directing that a thousand copies of the report be printed.

In the absence of the Chairman (Mr. Pieters) the report of the Committee on Ministerial Relief was read by Dr. Wyckoff. After careful consideration at several sessions of the Council action was taken as follows:— (1) That the report of the committee, together with a plan prepared by Mrs. MacNair, be printed and distributed

---

* See Annual Report for 1901, pages 6-8.
† Messrs. Landis, Winn, Pieters, Doughty.
‡ Messrs. Myers and Lampe.
§ See II following the Proceedings of the Council.

among the missions composing the Council; and that the several missions be requested to report their action in the matter to the next meeting of the Council through the committee of the Council. (2) That it is important that some uniform plan be adopted. (3) That any such plan should include also provision for Bible women.

The following report of the Committee on Lay Workers* was adopted, and the committee discharged:—

During month of May, a circular stating the object of the committee, and asking for information was sent to every member of the Council in any way connected with evangelistic work. To this circular only five replies have been received; but your committee has knowledge of other places than those reported by letter.

The information obtained from various sources shows:— (1) That much work, and that of considerable variety, is done by unpaid lay workers. (2) That in places where there are no pastors or evangelists, laymen are often able to keep the work from going back, but that in most cases they accomplish no more than that. (3) That there is very little if any systematic training of unpaid lay workers. (4) That the methods employed are in general not the result of definite plans, but such as suggest themselves at the time in connection with the work undertaken.

In the opinion of the committee it has reached the limit of its usefulness, and it requests to be discharged.

The Committee on the Distribution of Forces† reported that it had had no occasion to meet during the year and recommended that it be discharged. The report of the committee with its recommendation was adopted.

---

* Messrs. Fulton and Wyckoff.
† Messrs. MacNair, Winn, E. Rothesay Miller, Peeke, S. P. Fulton, Schneder and J. B. Hail.

4 NEW BUSINESS.

In view of the importance of the extension of Christianity in Japan at this time in its history as a nation, and in particular in view of its influential relations with the Continent of Asia, the Council adopted a resolution cordially inviting the Presbyterian Church of Canada to enter Japan and carry on work in connection with the Council.

The following letter from Mrs. Waddell, in response to the minute in memory of the Rev. Hugh Waddell adopted by the Council at its last meeting, was read.

> No. 6 Glandore Gardens,
> Antrim Road, Belfast,
> Oct. 2nd, 1901.
>
> To the Council of Missions of the
> Church of Christ in Japan.
>
> Dear friends: I desire to return to you very heartfelt thanks for your expression of sympathy with me and my family in this our time of sore bereavement.
>
> I thank you for the testimony you bear to my husband's long continued and faithful work for the cause of God in Japan. I also fervently pray and believe that the seed he was privileged to sow so abundantly, God will make to bear fruit.
>
> I remain, dear friends, yours in Christ,
> MARTHA WADDELL.

The following minute in memory of Mrs. Henry Stout was adopted.

Mr. Henry Stout was one of the oldest members of the Council. After long years of active service there came a time of sickness in which she could no longer continue that service; but none the less even to the end she was ever a constant stay to her husband and the other members of the mission to which she belonged. In her death the work of Christ in Japan has sustained a great loss.

The Council extends its cordial sympathy to her husband and daughter in their peculiar sorrow, and to the South Japan Mission of the Reformed Church in its loss of a valued member; and it commends them all in faith to the comfort of him who is the God of Comfort.

The following minute in memory of Dr. Geo. C. Needham was adopted.

The Council recalls with pleasure and gratitude the exceedingly helpful visit to Karuizawa of the Rev. Geo. C. Needham and Mrs. Needham. We who are members of the Council have been much helped by both the spoken and written words of Dr. Needham; and now that he has been taken to his reward, we desire to extend to Mrs. Needham our sincere sympathy in her bereavement, and to express our high appreciation of the character of Dr. Needham and of the great work done by him under God for men.

The Secretary was requested to write to Mr. Parrott and to express to him in the name of the Council its regret on learning of the loss sustained by the Bible Societies in consequent of the destruction of the Bible House by fire; and in particular to convey to him personally a message of Christian sympathy in the deep sorrow that has overtaken him.

A letter from A. Lawrence, Esq., giving as account of the work of the Bible Societies Committee in Japan, was read.*

---

* See Appendix.

A committee † was appointed to prepare a minute conveying to the Rev. James H. Ballagh the congratulations of the Council on his seventieth birthday. Following is the minute.

In the good providence of God, our brother James H. Ballagh, the oldest member of the Council, has reached his seventieth year. Two score and more years have been devoted to the cause of Christ in Japan.

We, hereby, place on record our thankfulness to God for his work, and our sincere appreciation of the long and arduous labors through which he has passed, and of the earnest zeal and devotion with which he has spent his life for the Japanese.

We heartily congratulate Mr. Ballagh upon the vigor and buoyancy with which he carries the weight of three score and ten years, and pray that he may be spared the infirmities of old age yet many years to enjoy the fruits of his untiring labors, and to see the work of the Lord prospering in this land.

The committee appointed to report regarding the advisability of holding, in connection with the Annual Meeting of the Council, a Conference for the consideration of topics directly connected with the spiritual life of the missionary, presented its report. This, with certain amendments, was adopted as follows:—

(1) The Council shall meet annually as hitherto. (2) A Conference shall be held every year as a part of the Council. (3) The several missions are recommended to endeavor to procure as large an attendance as possible at the meeting of the Council. (4) At each Annual Meeting of the Council a commitee shall be appointed to prepare a program for the next Annual Meeting. (5) The next Annual Meeting of the Council shall be held at Arima.

---

† Messrs. Booth and Brokaw.

The following resolutions were adopted :—

1. That a summary of the Proceedings of the Conference held in connection with the present meeting of the Council be included in the Annual Report of the Council.*

2. That the Rev. E. Rothesay Miller be requested to address a letter to the Synod suggesting the propriety of requiring that in cases of marriage by ministers of the Church the legal residence of the bride be regularly transferred ; and also that he urge upon the Synod the importance of inducing members changing their residence to connect themselves with the churches in the places to which they remove.

Dr. A. D. Hail and the Rev. H. B. Price were appointed the Committee of Arrangements for the next meeting of the Council.

The Rev. H. V. S. Peeke was appointed to prepare the next General Report of the Work of the Year.

The Council expressed its thanks to the Karuizawa Church for the use of its building and other courtesies ; and also to the Rev. E. Rothesay Miller, the retiring President, for his faithful and efficient services, and requested him to offer a copy of his sermon to the *Fukuin Shimpo* for publication.

On the recommendation of the Committee on Nominations, the following appointments for the coming year were made :—

President, Dr. Stout ; Vice President, Dr. Schneder ; Secretary, Mr. H. W. Meyers ; Treasurer, Mr. E. Rothesay Miller.

Publications Committee : William Imbrie, E. Rothesay

---

* See Appendix.

Miller, M. N. Wyckoff, W. B. McIlwaine, T. M. MacNair, A. D. Hail, H. K. Miller.

Committee on Statistics: H. M. Landis, T. C. Winn, A. Pieters, H. W. Meyers, C. Noss, H. Brokaw.

Committee on Program: T. C. Winn, A. D. Hail, H. B. Price.

The minutes were read and adopted; Dr. Rankin in a brief address expressed to the Council the pleasure which his presence at its sessions had afforded him; the doxology was sung; and after prayer and the benediction by Dr. Rankin, the Council adjourned to meet at Arima on the first Wednesday in September 1903.

II

GENERAL REPORT OF THE WORK OF THE YEAR

BY THE
REV. H. M. LANDIS

The last report of this Council is entitled the "Twenty-fourth Annual Report of the Council of Missions Coöperating with the Church of Christ in Japan." It is therefore proper that we give a thought to this meeting as the twenty-fifth anniversary of our body,—not exactly twenty-six annual meetings of our body however, nor exactly twenty-five years, since the first meeting. On referring to the records we find the first meeting dated May 19th, 1876, and entitled "Meeting of Conference between the Japan Missions of the Presbyterian and Reformed Churches in the U. S. A." It was called by invitation of the Presbyterian Mission; and the members present are given as Dr. J. C. Hepburn, Rev. Messrs. Thompson, Green, Imbrie, and Mr. J. C. Ballagh of the Presbyterian Mission ; Rev. Dr. S. R. Brown, and Rev. Messrs. J. H. Ballagh, Stout and Miller, of the Ref. Mission. The business was the question of the feasibility and desirability of uniting the churches under the care of these two missions into a common presbytery. Before this meeting however the Presbytery of the churches under the pastoral care of Messrs. Thompson and Ballagh had appointed a committee (Messrs. Thompson and Miller) to confer and prepare "Standards of Church Government and Doctrine." Moreover the United Presbyterian Mission of Scotland was to be invited to come into the union. It was also agreed that in the event of the formation of a common presbytery, it would be advisable to have an annual meeting of the members of the different missions at which duplicate reports could be prepared to be sent home." "After the expression of pleasure and thankfulness for the harmony that had marked the conference and the hope of the realization of its plans," this first meeting of the Council was adjourned. The United Presbyterian Mission's attitude may be indicated by the opening sentence of its letter of May 24th, 1876 accepting the invitation to union,— "We have received your letter of the 16th with nothing but pleasure and we contemplate with great satisfaction the idea of having only one Presbyterian Church in Japan." Messrs. Waddell and McLaren were the appointees on the joint committee.

The second meeting takes place just five weeks later, June 21, and it is not one of the annual meetings recommended. It met especially to receive, discuss and adopt the report on standards of government and doctrine.

The standards of doctrine adopted were the Canons of the Synod of Dort, the Westminster Confession of Faith and Shorter Catechism, and the Heidelberg Catechism.

The Form of Government of the Presbyterian Church in the U. S. A. was taken as the basis of government and adapted by various omissions and additions.

The record gives forty-two pages to the minutes of this meeting; and this fact alone serves to show the careful and earnest work accomplished.

The third meeting held June 21, 1877, just a year after the second meeting, seems to have been regarded the meeting yielding the first Annual Report; but even if so, to call the report rendered at this meeting of 1902, the Twenty-fifth Annual Report, still involves an error of one, as this present report would on this count be the Twenty-sixth Annual Report.

At this third meeting of the Council, a few further amendments were added to the work of the previous year on the Standards of Doctrine and Government; arrangements were made for the meeting of the united presbytery (called Chukwai) and a committee was appointed to report on educational work. The fourth council meeting Sep. 17, 1877 gives us as the result of this the Union Theological School first located in Tsukiji and now connected with the Meiji Gakuin.

Accordingly on Oct. 8, 1877, a presbytery meeting was held (Rev. D. Thompson, Moderator) which consummated the union of the three churches of the Presbyterian order in Japan, under the name "The Union (later called United) Church of Christ in Japan,—Nippon Kirisuto Itchi Kyokwai." Thus was realized the hope of May 1876, that "a plan might be devised by which they (the various Presbyterian and Reformed Missions and their Japanese colaborers) could become fellow-laborers in a common presbytery (or classis) not connected ecclesiastically with any foreign body, and which would receive the warm approval of the home churches." In the work to this end however no "principles of presbyterial church government were abandoned, for it was not at all intended to found a new denomination."

Nine organized churches were connected with this first Union Presbytery, reporting a membership of 623, and three Japanese ministers,—Messrs. Okuno, Ogawa and Toda,—were ordained.

This much only is given here to remind us at this so called 25th anniversary of the beginnings of this Council and of the Church with which this Council coöperates, constituted just 25 years ago next Oct. 3rd.*

DR. IMBRIE:—"To every thoughtful mind whatever may be counted on to leave its mark upon the history of a nation can not but be of interest; and to none is this more so than to those who hold it for foundation truth that God reigns. Therefore it is by no mere accident that the Annual Reports of the Council are wont at least to touch upon events of national moment occurring during the year under review. And how many such events there have been since the time of the organization of the Council, or from a time shortly previous!

---

* *Note.*—The Ger. Ref. Mission,—invited February 9th, 1884. No official answer was received January 21st, '85; sympathy and purpose to unite were expressed December 4th, '85 and asked to consider the extensive work centering in Sendai; secured permission to enter Council April 22nd,' 86 and requested to take up work in Sendai. S. Presb. Mission,—invited September 29th, 1885 on hearing of their coming to Japan; suggested to them to undertake the great work opening in the Western provinces and that centering in Sendai; entered December 4th, 1885, by introduction of Messrs. Grinnan and MacAlpine; invited to visit Kochi and Nagoya in hope of finding a permanent residence in one of these places. The Womans Mission Union requested to present statistics to be entered into the annual report, January 25th, '86, in recognition of their services to the Union Church. Cumb. Presb. Mission,—organic union with the United Church of Christ concluded, and the C. P. Mission cordially welcomed to membership in the Council, January 16th, 1890; earlier negotiations (May 27th, '82) were dropped until circumances should change or new proposals be made.

The opening of the country to foreign intercourse after two centuries of strict exclusion; the restoration of the Emperor to actual sovereignty; the introduction of the railroad, the telegraph, the newspaper, and other like instruments of material and intellectual progress; the national constitution and the beginning of constitutional government; new codes of law, criminal and civil; the war with China; the revision of the treaties and the admission of Japan to a place of equality among the nations; the recent crisis in China and the new place of prestige and influence gained by Japan through the course which she pursued. That is a wonderful series of events. No one can truly say that the reports of this Council contain matter of little general interest. We missionaries to Japan have seen strange things; and so many of them. Scarcely a year has passed without something happening really worthy of record."

The most noteworthy political event perhaps is the Anglo-Japanese Alliance to maintain the status quo of the East especially of China and Korea. The fact that this is the first alliance of an Oriental and non-Christian nation with a European and Christian nation, made as it is too with the foremost naval power and with the one whose mission work along with that of the U. S., practically covers Protestant mission efforts in Japan, moreover the fact that the alliance is not only made to uphold peace, but a peace demanded by every claim of right and by every consideration of humanity and of the world's commerce,—all such—like advantages, ought to be regarded as in line with the moral tone of Christianity, and may well incline people's minds to a favorable consideration of Christ's own kingdom of righteousness and peace. Many too will find a new incentive for the study of English and thus get the key to a noble Christian literature, and to direct intercourse with the most Christian of nations.

The present apparent results of this alliance are two: A new friendliness for England and the things for which England and America stand; and a new determination to prove a force to be depended on in any contingency that may arise. To what in the end the alliance may lead no one can foretell. It may be a great peace, and it may be a great war.

Japan's readiness to arbitrate the House Tax in the Concessions ought to give assurance of the Government's desire to meet the utmost claims of equity as well as to suit the convenience of the stranger sojourning within the Empire's borders.

Dr. IMBRIE.—" Among the things deserving of notice in a record of the work of the year is the formation by a number of the missions composing the Council of corporations for the holding of property. This has been done under Article 34 of the Civil Code which reads as follows:—

'Associations or trusts founded for religious worship or teaching, for charity, for education or for art, or for any other purpose beneficial to the public, and the object of which is not to make a profit out of the conduct of their business, may on obtaining permission from the proper authorities be made juridical persons.'

Those who are acquainted with the former status of foreigners in Japan know that the formation of such corporations has been possible only since the new treaties have come into effect. Before that time real estate, outside of the so called Foreign Settlements, could be held only by Japanese subjects; and even since that time the difficulties in the way of obtaining the sanction of the authorities required by the Article quoted have been greater than would perhaps be expected. To go into details would occupy more space than can properly be afforded in this report. It may however be said that on two points especially the authorities have been most particular:—

1 Corporations of this kind are not ecclesiastical organizations; and they are not, as corporations, to perform ecclesiastical functions. Their powers as *corporations* are limited to the " holding and management of land, buildings and other property ;" though this property may be used " for the extension of Christianity, the carrying on of Christian education, and the performance of works of charity and benevolence."

2 Corporations of this kind must be composed of missionaries *residing in Japan* and *associating themselves together as individuals.* The authorities do not object to such corporations receiving grants of funds from Boards of Foreign Missions in foreign countries; nor do they object to the selling of property and returning the proceeds of sales to such Boards; but they will not allow anything to enter any Articles of Association that can be construed as giving Boards of Foreign Missions legal control of the corporations, or as conferring upon them legal standing as corporations in Japan.

But while the laws of Japan do not permit the Boards of Foreign Missions to hold property in Japan, the sanction of these corporations composed of missionaries residing in Japan furnishes a simple and secure method for the holding of land and other property, and one which so far as appears is satisfactory to the Boards themselves."

We well remember how like a clap of thunder out of a clear sky came the Imperial Rescript on Private Schools promulgated Aug. 3rd, 1899 to go into force the next day and without any apparent reason depriving especially mission schools of privileges recently granted, and threatening to disturb most seriously their educational prospects. The recent rescript on the exchanges is another instance of the kind. Without arguing now bearings in law and equity, such instances show very clearly how legislation in Japan is an ellipse with two foci, one located in Parliament subject to the Imperial veto power, visible, responsible and calculable, the other less easily located, arbitrary, irresponsible and incalculable beforehand. Thus Japan tries to combine modern politics with the more ancient Asiatic traditions, and it will be of interest to watch which tendency is to conquer, though most will feel that modern ideas will here too be victorious as in so many other places.

A year ago some one wrote, "The battle for religious liberty in Japan has been fought and won for all time to come. Two years ago it seemed lost. The Department of Education struck a deathblow at Christian education when it forbade religious teaching in 'recognized' schools.———Now however all is changed. The Department of Education while acceding fullest religious liberty has restored to our academy graduates (a mission school) equal privileges of admission to higher institutions with graduates from government schools of the same grade, and in addition, privileges new and unexpected; the graduates of our college (higher course) are granted licenses by the government for teaching English in schools of academic grade, and our students are exempted from military conscription. Japan has officialy passed upon Christian Education and has pronounced *approved.*" But lo, the unexpected occurs again, and again that invisible, incalculable, arbitrary locus began a few months ago to describe an unknown curve just as our schools after much and painstaking effort thought they were emerging from the labyrinth of red tape into the light and liberty promised a year ago. "Thus on account of this recent order from the

Educational Department, according to which candidates from private or mission schools must first upon payment of a special fee take a preliminary examination covering the whole five years Middle School course before they can apply for examinations to the government High Schools, many are again deterred from coming to us and some even feel obliged to change their plans for life. This recent order works great injustice; it takes away again the very privilege for which Christian schools contended when suddenly deprived a few years ago and which had been granted again a year ago. Thus Christian schools are again discriminated against. They are again agitating however, making also strong representations to the Educational Department and there is some hope that these may again be crowned with success."

DR. IMBRIE:—"Those who have followed the history of Christian work in Japan during recent years will remember that in 1899 there was issued under the authority of the Minister of Education what is known as Instruction No. 12; an order which forbade all teaching of religion and all religious services in schools having government recognition. This forced all those who hold to the principle that schools carried on by Christian missions should be Christian institutions, to surrender government recognition along with its attendant privileges. After long earnest efforts, while Instruction No. 12 was allowed to stand unchanged, regulations were issued by which the graduates of such schools as the Meiji Gakuin were allowed precisely the same privileges as the graduates of the government Middle Schools, though the schools were not allowed to bear the name Middle School (*Chu Gakko*).

That concession on the part of the Department of Education was understood to be and was accepted as a final settlement of the question; but during the spring of this year new regulations were issued requiring the graduates of all schools excepting the government Middle Schools to pass a special examination in addition to the examination required of the graduates of the government Middle Schools in order to enter the Higher Schools (*Koto Gakko*.) Also a special fee of 5 *yen* was to be paid for this previous examination.

Shortly after these new regulations were issued Messrs. Ibuka, Honda, and Kataoka laid the case before the authorities and endeavored to obtain relief. Also a letter was addressed to the Minister of Education, signed by representatives of the Meiji Gakuin,

Aoyama Gakuin, Tohoku Gakuin, and Doshisha. This letter was designed to bring the matter to the attention of Baron Kikuchi from the point of view of foreigners deeply interested in the welfare of the institutions affected by the regulations; and as it presents a somewhat full statement of the case it is here inserted.

"To His Excellency Baron Dairoku Kikuchi.

Dear Baron Kikuchi:

We beg leave to address you as American missionaries representing a large number of Christians in America, who are deeply interested in the Meiji Gakuin, Aoyama Gakuin, Tohoku Gakuin, Doshisha, and similar institutions in Japan.

About a year ago regulations were issued under which the graduates of such schools as these were permitted to enter Koto Gakko on precisely the same terms as the graduates of Chu Gakko: a privilege long hoped for and highly prized. Recently however this privilege has been seriously curtailed by a new set of regulations. Before applying for permission to pass the competitive examination for admission to Koto Gakko, the graduates of these schools must first pass a special preliminary examination on all the subjects included in the Chu Gakko curriculum.

To the students who have just graduated from these schools, as well as to those who have entered upon the last year of the course and who can not now without difficulty change their school connection, this is a real hardship. It is also a manifest injury to the schools themselves. Last year their graduates had the same privileges as those of Chu Gakko; now they have not the same. But there is another point which we beg leave to urge upon your consideration. The regulations issued last year had a history behind them; they were the result of a long series of negotiations.

In 1899 what is known as Instruction No. 12 was issued under the sanction of the Minister of Education. Prior to that time a number of the schools above mentioned had been granted Chu Gakko licenses; but as Instruction No. 12 forbade all religious instruction and services, "even outside the regular course of instruction," they were forced to surrender such licenses. This was because the funds by which these schools were founded and with which they had been carried on had been given upon the distinct understanding that they were always to be Christian institutions. Under these circumstances to retain their licenses would have been to betray their trust.

In the hope of obtaining relief, a petition was presented to the Minister of Education. The Minister of Education, the Minister of Foreign Affairs, the Prime Minister, all kindly gave interviews to the petitioners; and when it appeared improbable that the original petition could be acceded to, another request was submitted. This was essentially the same plan as that embodied in the regulations issued last year; and regarding this the Minister of Education stated that he thought that in time it might be accepted. Months passed; from time to time inquiry was made; the information received gave grounds for continued hope. At last the regulations of last year were issued.

In view of all this, those in charge of these schools thought they had good reason for believing that the position of the schools, upon compliance with such instructions as the Department of Education might see fit to give, would be assured. The schools were visited by inspectors, and whatever changes or additions were declared necessary, were cheerfully made. The new conditions were made public, and thereupon the number of students rapidly increased. The friends of the schools in America were informed of the new state of things, and preparations were making for the improvement of the schools. In one case, for example, the annual grant of funds for current expenses was increased by eight hundred yen; and fifteen thousand yen which had been held in trust until the prospects of the school should warrant their expenditure, were granted for the erection of a new building.

Taking all these facts into consideration, you will not we think regard it strange that the issuing of the recent regulation was a cause of very great disappointment and surprise; and we beg of you most earnestly to form some plan which shall restore to such schools as these the privilege granted last year after so much effort.

Reference has been made to Instruction No. 12. If that Instruction could be restricted in its application to schools supported by public funds, it would then be possible for the schools which we represent to become Chu Gakko; and that would render any special arrangement on their behalf unnecessary. No doubt directly after the Instruction was issued, there were great difficulties in the way of such a restriction;

but it has been our constant hope that the time would come when those difficulties would be no longer insuperable. We trust that that time is now approaching.

In conclusion we may be permitted to express what is our firm conviction on two points.

1 We believe that such schools as these, if only they receive such kindly encouragement as the Department of Education may properly afford them, will establish themselves as permanent institutions of great value to Japan in the education of her boys and young men.

2 We believe also that the restriction of Instruction No. 12 to such schools as are supported by *public* funds; and the granting to such schools as are supported by *private* funds, but which are recognized as doing the work of Chu Gakko, the rank of Chu Gakko together with the right of religious freedom in education, would do more than is commonly supposed still further to strengthen the feeling of friendship for Japan already so strong in England and America.'

Regarding the outcome of these efforts it is of course impossible now to speak with certainty. This however may be said: That in important particulars conditions have changed since Instruction No. 12 was issued; that the attitude of all those in authority who have been approached has been one of evident appreciation of the reasonableness of the claims urged; that the Minister of Education has kindly promised to give the matter due consideration; and that there are good grounds for hoping that a settlement of the question will be reached more satisfactory than the former one. It is however not to be forgotten that there are peculiar difficulties in the way which it may take some little time to surmount."

To this account of the matter given by Dr. Imbrie may be added the significant reply of one of our Japanese educators who when asked by the editor of the Woman's Work for Woman, Miss Parsons, what he regarded as the chief hindrance to our educational work, promptly replied "The Educational Department."

A sensation of the year was Prof. T. Inoue's proposition to found a new religion, a proposition which even such a genius as Napoleon the Great once ventured to suggest—viz. the need of a new religion—to his savants who amid the upheavals of the French Revolution were busy in trying to remove the debris, Christianity among the rest. "All right," replied one of the savants or words to that effect, "Your

Majesty will submit to be crucified and rise again the third day, and then we will proceed to formulate the new religion." Supercilious haughteur and unblushing self-sufficiency may even yet characterize a professor of philosophy in the Imperial University of Tokyo. But the sensation passes as many another of its kind.

The Perry monument unveiled July 14, at Kurihama under the auspices of the Beiyu Kyokwai (American Association in Japan, Baron Kaneko, Ex-Minister of Justice and sometime Japanese Minister at Washington, being President), to celebrate the semi-centennial of Commodore Perry's landing in Japan July 14th, 1853, called forth notable expressions of friendship and esteem between Japan and the United States her best and uniformly unselfish friend. "Such a graceful act will go far toward perpetuating the good-will which exists, and ought always to exist, between Japan and the United States."

The Tokyo University for Women, opened last fall under Principal Naruse, a Christian, ought to mark an important milestone in the progress of woman's uplifting in this Empire. The five hundred pupils enrolled at the opening will make themselves heard in due time. The twentieth century promises thus great things for Japan's women, and let us hope this and similar signs may prove heralds for other parts of the Orient.

Two agitations of the recent past form healthy tokens of Japan's humane progress. The one is the effort to rescue woman from the worst of slavery in connection with the social evil, an effort crowned by special regulations issued by the Home Department providing "Jiyu haigyo" (free cessation), viz. the privilege to unfortunates in brothels to leave a hateful business without interference by their taskmasters. Unfortunately the Courts of Law have not seen their way clear to declare the financial contract null and void in every sense. (See Mrs. Pierson's last suggestion at the end of this Report.)

The agitation in favor of the unfortunate sufferers from the poisonous Ashio copper mines took on grand proportions last winter. The government too through the Tokyo University (Agriculture Dept.) has scientifically investigated the reasons for complaint and found them substantiated, but so far no equally substantial relief has been heard from as far as the writer is aware. A graduate of the Meiji Gakuin took part in the extensive work done in Komaba in investigating this serious cause of complaint.

The Aomori disaster in which over two hundred soldiers lost their lives in a snow storm, aroused genuine sympathy and humane efforts to assuage the griefs of those left behind.

The 15th meeting of the Daikwai, held in Tokyo, October 11-14, was specially characterized by a strong evangelistic spirit. Twice the Synod went into a committee of the whole to discuss evangelistic methods, and to determine the attitude to be taken toward the Taikyo Dendo movement (often in Eng. referred to as the 20th Cent. Forward Movement). While it was felt that the Japan Evangelical Alliance was not altogether adapted to an evangelistic campaign, yet the spirit and aim of its forward movement met with approval from all, and it was felt that the Church should more fully awake to evangelistic zeal. In this spirit the Synod's Board of Missions was reorganized, the time having come for putting it on a more permanent basis. Hon K. Kataoka, M.P. was chosen as the official head of the Board consisting of ten directors, and such officers as these directors may appoint.

The election of Hon. K. Kataoka more recently as President of the Doshisha is to be noted. As several other members of our Church are found in the faculty of the Doshisha, as Dr. Alexander too for a time slighty contributed to its teaching staff, we may see signs that the Doshisha is progressing towards a fulfilment of an ideal many hold for it,—an undenominational Christian university, by making it interdenominational in its work through calling the best men to its chairs regardless of denominational affiliations.

During the winter a popular meeting for deepening the interest in the Board of Mission's efforts and especially also for receiving special contributions, was called to meet at the President's official residence as Speaker of the Lower House of the Diet. About 150 responded to this kind invitation and nearly 1000 yen were subscribed at this meeting, making it is hoped a good gain on contributions of past years.

DR. IMBRIE:—"The work of the Board of Missions of the Church of Christ in Japan (*Dendo Kyoku*) is under the general direction of the Synod, and is carried on independently of the Council of Missions. It is however a work in whose success the Council is deeply interested, and a general account of it may properly form a part of the Annual Report of the Council.

In the month of February the East Japan Mission of the Presbyterian Church received the following communication:—

'At a special meeting of the Executive Committee of the Board of Missions of the Church of Christ in Japan held yesterday (January 30th) the following resolutions were adopted: —

Inasmuch as there seems to be a special opening for work among the increasing number of Japanese in Shinchiku, Taichu, Tamsui, and other cities in Formosa, from which frequent calls come to this committee; and inasmuch as the Board of Missions (*Dendo Kyoku*) is unable at present to undertake new work in those places in addition to that which it is now carrying on, resolved:

1 That this committee earnestly recommend and invite the East Japan Mission of the Presbyterian Church to open work in Formosa in coöperation with the Board of Missions of the Church of Christ in Japan.

2 That this committee recommend to the mission that one of its members visit Formosa and investigate the field; and that if possible he do so in company with Mr. Uemura who expects to leave for Formosa in about a fortnight.'

The mission on considering this communication decided to request the Board of Foreign Missions of the Presbyterian Church in the U. S. A. to make a special grant of funds sufficient to meet the expenses of such a visit later in the year. The Board, while unable at the time to make a special appropriation for the purpose, sanctioned such a visit in case the necessary funds could be transferred from some other item in the appropriations for the present fiscal year. In view of these facts the mission at its meeting in May appointed a committee to confer with the Executive Committee of the Board (*Dendo Kyoku*) regarding the prosecution of work in Formosa. Such a conference will be held in the early autumn.

The reasons influencing the Executive Committee in making this proposition to the mission briefly stated are two:—

1 In no part of the empire is there at present to be found a more promising field for Christian work than among the Japanese settling in Formosa who now number 33120 according to the statistics of 1899 as given by Goto Shimpei, Civil Governor of Formosa, in a recent article in the Independent. So far as mere numbers are concerned this may not be very impressive; but the importance and promise of the field are to be seen rather in the character of the immigrants and the general situation. In certain important particulars the conditions

in Formosa resemble those in the Hokkaido. There is the same enterprise, and the same breaking away from old surroundings and old prejudices. Relatively also there is a large number of Christians who are earnestly inviting the Executive Committee to carry on work among them and with them. To this it may be added that exceptional opportunities are afforded to meet with officials and with officers in the army temporarily there on duty who will carry the knowledge of Christianity they may gain wherever else they may go.

2 The Board of Missions has been foremost in the field, and already has a good work well begun. It has two churches, one of which supports its pastor and the other promises to raise twenty yen a month. Besides these churches there are a number of groups of Christians which give every promise of growing into churches. In a peculiar sense therefore Formosa belongs to the Church of Christ in Japan; and it is the earnest desire of its Board of Missions that it be more extensively occupied by it. But to do this it must have help. Therefore the invitation of the Executive Committee to the mission.*

The special purpose of Mr. Uemura in his visit during the early spring was the organization of a church at Tainan, the congregation there defraying the expenses of his journey. That special errand however was made the occasion of a general visitation to most of the places in which the Board (*Dendo Kyoku*) has work. On his return he gave an account of his journey to the Executive Committee that seemed to more than one who heard it like a chapter from the Acts.

Two days he spent at Keelung the northeast port of the island which reminded him of Yokohama when he was a boy, in its bustle, its incongruities and its things not to be named; but with this great difference, that he found there a group of Christians awaiting his arrival, who welcomed him and would hardly let him go without a promise to send them a pastor for whose support they promised twenty yen a month. For three days he was in Taihoku. There besides preaching in the church he gave a lecture in the public hall—an interesting meeting at which some three hundred were present, and of which a full account appeared in the daily papers.

---

* It may also be said that the extensive work of the Canadian Presbyterians in the north, and the English Presbyterians in the South of the island adds peculiar force to this point.—(Landis).

He held also two special meetings; one for women, and one for young men who invited him to speak to them at their club. From there he visited two other places in which Mr. Kawai the pastor of the church at Taihoku has been carrying on services regularly, one three hours distant by rail and the other somewhat off the line. There also the people are ready to pay ten yen a month. Taking ship from Tamsui on the north-west coast he went south to Ampi, the port of Tainan and a place beautiful for situation, stopping by the way at the Pescadores. At Ampi, greatly to the surprise of both, he met an old friend, a captain of *gens d'armes*, a Christian man who invited him to his office where he arranged for a meeting composed of his men and others. From Ampi he went to Tainan, where he saw the English Presbyterian missionaries; and after organizing the church, which promises twenty yen a month towards the support of a pastor, returned to Taihoku overland by a construction train. From Taihoku he went once more to Tamsui where he held a meeting that lasted until late in the evening.

It was a hard trip, and when it was ended he was nearly tired out. But there were two things that constantly impressed him and made him forget his weariness. Everywhere he went men were ready to listen. It is not that the natural man ceases to be a natural man when he goes to Formosa; but in Formosa there are many intelligent men of inquiring minds, who being without the thousand and one things to attract attention in Japan, have ears to hear. The other thing that constantly impressed him was the fact that wherever he went he met with Christians. Even on the treeless Pescadores he found a little company.

The second matter of special interest connected with the Board of Missions is an invitation recently received from China. There is now in Tientsin a considerable number of Japanese Christians; officers and soldiers in the army, men engaged in trade or service of various kinds; and among them Major Hibiki. At a meeting of the Executive Committee held a few weeks ago a letter from these Christians was presented requesting that Mr. Ibuka or Mr. Uemura be sent to visit and organize a church among them— they meeting all the expenses of the journey. Whether it will be best to organize a church immediately is not yet decided, but it was agreed that the invitation to visit Tientsin should be accepted. Mr.

Uemura hopes to go, though he also has to be present at the meeting of evangelists and others to be held in the Hokkaido during the summer. The direct object of the visit, as already said, is to meet with the Japanese Christians and it may be to organize a church. But both among the Christians in Tientsin and among the members of the Executive Committee the question is asked, Who can tell whether this may not be a stepping-stone to foreign mission work in China? A question that can not but cause thoughts to arise in the mind when one regards the many indications that China is already looking to Japan for light."

The Synod made a note of the fortieth anniversary of Rev. J. H. Ballagh's arrival as missionary in Japan. This anniversary on November 11th, afforded an enthusiastic occasion for many of his co-workers, the fruit in good part of his labors, to assemble and make congratulatory addresses in the Kaigan Church, Yokohama. Such an occasion calls for more than a passing word of thanks and cheer, especially as Mr. Ballagh in God's good providence is still vigorous and may be good for many a year of effort for his Master. The confessions of the intense hatred felt in those early days toward the foreigner and his religion, were an impressive testimony to the power of divine grace to melt the prejudiced heart. Their chief ground for gratitude was that he by his transparent honesty, his devout and prayerful spirit and his intense devotion and personal sympathy, had awakened in them a sense of worship (*i.e.* worth-ship) of the true God, a thing then unknown to the Japanese spirit.

The committee on a theological periodical appointed by Council a year ago had some earnest and careful deliberation on the subject. Its subcommittee will have a report for this Council which may be trusted to lead to fruitage in appropriate action towards launching what is apparently needed to fill a great lack in the lives of the preachers, elders and intelligent members of our church generally.

A suggestion from Mr. Peeke along a somewhat different line calls for insertion here.

Why cannot we have a "Council Gazette" or some similarly named medium of communication such as the A. B. C. F. M. ("Mission News") and M. E. ("Tidings from Japan") people have. We are as many as they (in fact more), as handsome and as good. We need to have just such an organ as they. First get every Council missionary to subscribe, then get a certain number to promise one, two or three communications during the year. After that have some good fellow and the Kyobunkwan perhaps do the rest,—very simple, is it not? Some results (at least partly so) of the Tokyo Missionary Conference call for chronicling here.

1 First to be mentioned is the work which is almost ready to be given to the Church, viz. the uniform translation (and tunes) of 100 (or 125) standard hymns, and the Union Hymnal. The Nippon Seikokwai (Epise.) alone of the larger Protestant bodies does not join in the Union Hymnal, but a month or more ago published a new hymnal, introducing however the 125 standard hymns in the work. Quoting from Mr. MacNair's report;—This work (of the Union Hymnal) has made such progress during the year that the book should be ready for the press in early autumn. Four mission and church groups are taking part in it, namely, 1st, the Nihon Kirisuto Kyokwai and the Council coöperating therewith, 2nd, the Congregationalists with the Kumiai Churches, 3rd, the Methodists as represented by the Methodist Publishing House, and the Canadian Mission, and 4th, the Baptists and the Disciples combining to form one group. The Revision Committee consists of 12 members, three from each group; though the larger part of the work is done by a subcommittee of four persons of whom I am one.

The new book will contain 450 Hymns including the 125 "Kyotsu Sambika" (Uniform Hymns) which were completed by the middle of last year.

2 The Standing Committee of Coöperating Missions, has been formed as recommended by the Tokyo Missionary Conference. Mr. MacNair writes; "Since the last meeting of the Council the plan for the formation of an Intermission Standing Committee on Co-öperation has been approved by the required two-thirds majority of the missionaries. This committee was organized in January at a meeting of representatives held in the Y. M. C. A. parlors in Tokyo. None of the Episcopalian Missions voted in favor of the project; but all the other Protestant bodies except one or two of the smaller ones, sent delegates. Neither the Roman or Greek Catholics were invited to participate, nor were the Germans or the Universalists. Five of the twenty or more members of the committee are from the several missions composing this Council."

(A copy of the minutes of the first meeting, the only one held thus far, is found in the Japan Evangelist, January 1902.)

Instructive contributions to the literature of church union are the following: A paper by Dr. Alexander at a meeting of the Miss. Assoc. of Central Japan and published in the Japan Evangelist, (Japan Evangelist, May, 1901). A call by the same Association and seconded from Tokyo by leading missionaries (Japan Evangelist, June, 1901). A letter on union by the Bishops of the N. S. K. (Episcopal Church) and supplemented by Bishop Fyson (Japan Evangelist, July, 1901 and Tokyo Mission Conference Report.) Correspondence between Dr. Greene and Mr. Cholmondeley and another Episcopal clergyman given in Mission News of July and November, 1901,—a frank statement revealing the hopelessness of coming to anything like union between the Episcopal and other Protestant bodies and aptly illustrating the maxim that a person often speaks loudest of the virtues which he feels lacking.

Bishop Fyson is one of the strongest factors for Church union in the Anglo-Episcopal Church, low-church in his views, very friendly with all evangelical workers, and with clergy under him with whom it is a delight for others to work. He in conjunction with Rev. Walter Andrews and others, organized a union conference in Hakodate for foreign missionaries and united devotional meetings for all workers Japanese, and foreign in the Hokkaido; much enthusiasm was shown in the first meetings last Fall. The uniqueness of these meeting lay in their inclusiveness so forming a marked chapter in the history of Christian union in Japan. A second similar conference is to be held from August 14-19 this year.

One resolution of this Hokkaido conference deserves, on account of its practical nature, to be quoted,—" In order to promote in all their fulness the advantages of mission comity and economy, it was resolved that the present distribution of work be accepted and that henceforth no town or village of less than 5000 inhabitants already occupied by one mission be entered by another without consulting with the missionary already in charge."

Moreover a standing committee of reference on this and allied subjects consisting of one resident member of each mission was appointed.

3 Taikyo Dendo. This special evangelistic movement had its

inception with the Fukuin Domeikwai, but on request the Tokyo Missionary Conference coöperated through a committee, and hence it may be classed in so far as another result of that Conference.

For an account of Taikyo Dendo Methods in Tokyo, reference is here made to Dr. Imbrie's account in last year's printed Council Report not only because of its careful preparation but also because it was an addition made after the last Council meeting and so not read here then.

This work and its result are characteristic of the past year. The individual reports refer to it in many cases. A summary is rather difficult here, nor is it perhaps desirable to attempt a complete catalogue. The statistics ought to reveal pretty definite results after deducting, say, the ordinary rate of increase. No doubt a great many indirect results on the church members in awakening them to new life and consecration and especially in reclaiming backsliders and in putting into renewed activity various forms of church life, cannot be catalogued by statistics. Renewed health and vigor in the spiritual life is not directly accessible to mathematics. Besides many inquirers have not gotten beyond the inquirer's stage though some may be expected to do so yet in the near future. Such too the statistical tables do not disclose. The statistics also come only to the close of 1901, while quite an ingathering has been experienced during the first half of 1902.

One general remark here: The reading of the individual reports leaves the impression that the most definite results in Taikyo Dendo have been attained in the Tokyo and Miyagi regions including the Hokkaido. The statistics in percentage of additions do not altogether confirm this. It is less clear though perhaps it may be said that in these regions too, and especially in Tokyo the work has been more actively and enthusiastically prosecuted with more attention to details and more effort to secure definite results. For several reasons this would naturally be so in the capital,—the higher organization of the work, the abundance of Japanese workers, the presence of mission schools which became such active centers of interest and coöperation and in which the spirit of enthusiasm wore a deep and healthy tone (the girls' schools deserve preeminent mention here), the location here of the central office of the Taikyo Dendo, the presence of Mr. Mott and Mr. Torrey whose systematic work (especially that of the former) centered here first and foremost, though not confined altogether to Tokyo, and finally the marked spirit and volume of united prayer.

The emphasis laid upon prayer not merely in theory but especially in practice, and also upon individual work with inquirers cannot be too highly valued as a prime essential in all such work.

The unity of all Christians has never received a stronger demonstration in this Empire. Before this united effort in Taikyo Dendo, all denominationalism was made to pale (i. e. among Protestants). Perhaps the strong attitude and lofty sentiment struck by the Tokyo Conference on church unity find in this point legitimate fruit. It is significant that special forward movements planned by individual churches, as for example by our own, could not survive the grander union movement, a fact lamented by individuals here and there indeed but necessary to guarantee the real health of Taikyo Dendo.

As stated above, in our Synod misgivings were expressed as to the policy of supporting the Fukuin Domei-kwai in its Taikyo Dendo, and this mainly on two grounds. 1. Practical and historical: For neither in its inception or constitution nor in its history up to 1900, did it contemplate direct work like Taikyo Dendo. Practical success beyond all other efforts ought effectually to answer this criticism. 2. Doctrinal: Was its doctrinal position secure enough to demand implicit confidence and coöperation, and could it definitely slough off all tendencies dangerous to a truly evangelical and so to a thoroughly spiritual life? Did it not in its catholic and irenical spirit open the doors to workers and even leaders who were either not clear or even negative on salient Christian doctrines, even fundamental ones like our Lord's divinity, the resurrection, the atonement; and would not such looseness in the end vitiate much of its work and in fact work destructively as radicalism inevitably tends to do?

Hence the late meeting of the Fukuin Domeikwai was necessarily a critical one, marking an epoch in its history. For it could not but betray the presence of two tendencies together with a mediating party,—this last too exceedingly well meaning no doubt but dangerous because its very irenic and evangelistic spirit gave it respectability. It wanted life not doctrine not remembering the vital dependence of healthy enduring life upon doctrine.

The result is clear. A distinctively evangelical (or if you please, orthodox) attitude was struck and that too without alienating any but the radically negative element, an element whose destructive tendencies have been all too evident the last decade,—destructive not only to peace and to evangelical doctrine but to the spiritual life itself. Significant and startling facts might be rehearsed in proof here if necessary. One report received on this question says: " The interest in the movement (Taikyo Dendo) has been materially increased by the action of the Evangelical Alliance taken at its meeting in April. The Alliance had been so closely identified with the union effort that in the minds of many it was held responsible for the fact that Unitarians were permitted to take part in it. For this reason the Alliance was asked to disclose its position regarding the deity of Christ, and upon the answer depended the further confidence of many in the organization as an agency for conducting evangelistic work. It was largely due to our Japanese brethren of the Church of Christ in Japan that this demand for a clear statement of belief was made. Happily the reply of the Alliance was conclusive on the side of orthodoxy and established the fact that notwithstanding the controversy which has been carried on in the religious press and in pulpit and platform addresses throughout the winter,—perhaps in some measure on account of the controversy,—the great majority of Christian believers are sound on this cardinal doctrine of our faith. It is not unlikely that as a further outcome of influence, largely Presbyterian, the Alliance will be so reconstructed in the near future that it will come to serve as a means for effecting a measure of church federation, possibly something more than that, in the direction of union. This would be a natural result of the union in spirit and effort that has characterized the Forward Movement to so remarkable an extent." The resolution passed by the Evangelical Alliance is to the effect that " by those holding evangelical principles we mean those who regard the Bible as the perfect rule both for our faith and practice, and believe that our Lord Jesus Christ, who came down to this world for men and for their salvation, is God." (Japan Evangelist, May, 1902, p. 170).

Without aspiring to be a prophet, one may yet indulge the hope that this decisive step will prove regulative of Christianity's future in Japan, that the high water of radicalism has passed and that though its wreckage of the faith of not a few who once aspired to leadership and seemingly legitimately, is to be deplored, yet it has served to disclose the Rock of Ages the more effectually on whom the Church is and will remain founded for time and eternity. Such a rock can alone be God. "Upon this rock will I build my church and the gates of hell shall not prevail againt it." "And other foundation can no man lay than that is laid, which is Christ Jesus."

The postponement of the revision of its constitution to a year hence will no doubt arouse the elements once more and the battle of the faith may have to be fought over again. However the gain thus-far is an earnest, a guarantee and bulwark that can not be easily assailed, still less easily overcome. Certainly church union and interdenominational fraternity can be secured on no other ground than the unequivocal affirmation of Christ's deity.

DR. IMBRIE:—"During the month of April the annual meeting of the *Fukuin Domei Kwai* was held in the City of Tokyo. The *Fukuin Domei Kwai*, or Evangelical Alliance as it is commonly spoken of in English, is an organization that has hitherto permitted in its membership very much greater latitude of religious belief than that expressed in the articles of the body generally known by the English name. Until comparatively recently however perhaps all or nearly all of its members could fairly be regarded as evangelical in the sense in which that word is used in the title Evangelical Alliance. But for some time that had ceased to be the case. The organization has included also an element that with all sincerity it may be, but none the less with great danger to the cause of Christianity in Japan has actively propagated by both voice and pen a form of belief that has for its foundation a subtle but no less real denial that Jesus Christ was God manifest in the flesh; a form of belief particularly plausible to men with Confucianism in their blood.

How long under ordinary circumstances things would have been allowed to drift along in this way one cannot say; but last year when the *Taikyo Dendo*, or Forward Movement as it is called, was organized under the general direction of the Alliance very soon friction developed. For while most of those active in the movement were evangelical, there were a number who clearly were not evangelical but who as being members in good and regular standing saw no valid reason why they also should not take part as speakers. This condition of affairs brought on a number of differences more or less sharp; notably in one district of Tokyo.

From the beginning a number of the Japanese ministers insisted that under such circumstances the Alliance was not a proper body to have the general direction of affairs; and at the meeting of the Synod of the Church of Christ in Japan (*Daikwai*) the question was raised. The Synod however took the position that the particular work then carried on would end with the year; that for it to take any action that could be construed as adverse to the Forward Movement would be sure to be misunderstood; and that the best plan was to wait until the meeting of the Alliance in the spring and then seek to obtain a clear declaration of its principles. A few days before the meeting of the Alliance, at the stated meeting of the Presbytery of Tokyo the whole subject was carefully considered and it was agreed to support the plan advocated at Synod.

The precise point at issue was whether the Alliance should proclaim itself clearly regarding Christ and the Scriptures; and there were of course two parties. On the side favoring such a proclamation the members of the Synod, with the exception of one minister and one elder, were a unit. With them stood most of the Methodists and Baptists, and also a number of individuals from other churches. Those in opposition were made up of two groups: Those who were themselves the advocates of unevangelical dogmas, and those who were unwilling to take any action that would exclude such from membership in the Alliance.

The question came up in the form of an amendment to the Constitution presented by what is known as the Central Committee. According to that amendment the purpose of the Alliance was to be the "promotion of closer fellowship among all churches holding principles commonly called evangelical; the formation of plans for united work; and the making known to society the spirit of Christianity." So there was added a note defining who were meant by "those holding evangelical principles." They were there described as "those who accept the Scriptures as a perfect rule of faith and conduct; and who believe that our Lord Jesus Christ, who for us men and for our salvation came down to earth, is God."

The discussion which followed was not theological but practical: *i.e.* the question debated was not the character of the Scriptures or the nature of Christ, but simply the advisability of amending the Constitution in the way proposed; though of course it was the theological questions involved, that gave to the discussion its deep interest and importance. When the vote was taken it was found to be eighty-one to forty-four in favor of the amendment; but as an amendment to the Constitution requires a majority of two-thirds the proposed amendment was lost.

But the majority in favor of the amendment was a very large one and was not willing to let the matter rest without some action that would express its mind. Therefore at the afternoon session the matter was brought forward once more though in a different form. A resolution was introduced, not as an amendment to the Constitution but simply as the action of the body, declaring that no one should be eligible to membership who denied the divinity of Christ. This resolution, after some discussion, was nearly or quite unanimously referred to a special committee to consider and report upon.

The next day was Sunday and on Monday morning the committee presented its report. After setting forth the necessity of making a public declaration regarding the position of the Alliance, owing to the fact that calls for such a declaration had come to the Central Committee from various quarters, and that if no such declaration were made the relation of the organization to the Forward Movement could not continue as before, the commitee recommended that a resolution be adopted, not as an amendment to the Constitution but simply as the action of the body, declaring the position of the Alliance to be evangelical, and defining evangelical as including the acceptance of the Scriptures as a perfect rule of faith and conduct," and "the belief that our Lord Jesus Christ, who for us men and for our salvation came down to earth, is God."

There were present on Monday a much larger number than on Saturday; both parties recognizing the importance of the point at issue. As the question had already been fully considered, it was decided by a large majority to take the vote without further discussion. The result was that one hundred and eighteen out of an attendance of one hundred and sixty-six voted in favor of the recommendation of the committee. The question of the revision of the Constitution was referred to a committee of ten to report to the next annual meeting. Of these ten three are missionaries; a large proportion and an evident proof of kindly confidence on the part of the committee on nominations which was composed exclusively of Japanese members of the Alliance.

Some it may be will ask, Why should so large a place in the Annual Report of the Council be given to the meeting of the Alliance? For two reasons. The action of the Alliance was a declaration on the part of a large number of representative men that a deep and not a shallow Christology is of vital importance to Christian faith and life; and among those representative men the ministers and elders of the Church of Christ in Japan were among the foremost."

The decision to continue Taikyo Dendo as before till the next year's conference, therefore calls for enthusiastic approval all over the Empire and under God's blessing the motto "—Our Land for Christ,"—will advance a stage nearer fulfilment during the coming year.

Mr. Mott's work last fall was of unusual importance. The National Conference of representative Y. M. C. A. workers was carefully planned and executed, including 11 Presidents of Christian schools, 80 delegates from 35 student and city Y. M. C. A's., 12 leading pastors and editors, &c. For four days these workers under Mr. Mott's lead conferred on the work with special reference to the evangelization of students during this high tide of opportunity. Direct evangelistic meetings followed in seven cities of the Empire giving a net result of 1464 inquirers with purpose to become "pupils of Christ,"—students among these numbering over 1000 and including 120 medical students, a class proverbially hard to reach and in Japan even more so. Mr. Mott also delivered addresses in government High Schools on the influence of Christianity among the students of the world, and is the first distinctively religious worker invited as such to speak inside the Tokyo University. Careful plans for conserving and extending this work so cordially in harmony with Taikyo Dendo were laid under Y. M. C. A. auspices, (Japan Evangelist, November, 1901).

In a complete record of religious work for the year, Dr. Torrey's visit and labors in Tokyo, Sendai, Nagoya, Kyoto, Osaka, Kobe, Yamaguchi, Saga and Nagasaki, with many deciding for Christ, would require notice. His view of the work is cheering,—"This land is ripe for a great harvest. I wish I could help for a year with the brethren."

Coming back now to the Forward Movement, an idea of its extent is given by the following figures for 1901 (as estimated). (Taikyo Dendo, January, 1902) (Japan Evangelist, February, 1902) (Tidings from Japan, February, 1902).

Provinces reached	42
Denominations taking part	22
Churches	376
Workers (native and foreign)	536
Handbills and posters distributed	2,004,250
Tracts and hymns	698,650
Contributions (yen)	10,742.82
* Inquirers (including converts)	15,440
Baptisms	1,181
Attendants upon services	359,275

(Recent results in 1902 thus far it may be possible to tabulate later). Some points to be noted about this revival are as follows:

1 It has been carried on in the churches by church members. That of nineteen years ago was in large halls.

2 The workers include men and women who stand high in society, several members of parliament, judges and other officials, many students, prominent merchants, &c.

3 At no time did enthusiasm exceed the bounds of decorum. Fanaticism is absent, and even opponents have created no unseeming disturbances. It has been consequently called a Presbyterian revival.

4 Street preaching has been approved and even facilitated by the police.

5 Great and many meetings, people packing the churches night after night as never before.

6 Widespread knowledge of Christian fundamentals so as to ensure intelligent attention and earnestness among inquirers.

7 Though evidently God's Spirit is working in these meetings they come as a fruitage from many years of faithful and prayerful labors of Japanese and foreign workers. (Japan Evangelist, July 1901) (Tidings from Japan, June, 1901).

8 The evident dependence on the Holy Spirit as manifested in the volume of prayer has already been referred to.

9 Japanese initiative and leadership, also personal work, generally

---

* It must of course be carefully remembered that by inquirers are meant not necessarily prospective Christians but only such as profess a desire to know more. The sad fact too must be stated that a small percentage of those who gave their names and addresses, thought only to play a practical joke by giving false addresses.

a heavy "cross" to Japanese, they giving unstintedly of their time, energy and even means.

10 The evangelical, personal, direct nature of the preaching,—not merely ethics or apologetics or Christian civilization,—but the cross and its meaning, "Christ and him crucified." " It has given fresh evidence that the truths best worth preaching are those that are distinctively Christian."—(*Imbrie*).

11 Its careful organization and wide extension,—Kyushu and the furthest limits of Hokkaido, cities and backwoods reached almost equally, and all classes aimed at.

12 In many cases converts who had heard for years, were now in this rising wave brought to decision.

13 An interesting fact is found in the finances. The original program for 1901 contemplated the raising of 5000 yen; the amount actually raised for 1901 was 10,472.821.

14 Even Buddhists waked up and followed with similar forward movements, famous priests arranging for special preaching services, marching the streets, visiting stores and houses. Such testimony from antagonists can be depended upon. Many priests attended these meetings and some are evidently impressed.

15 The work of and for children needs special mention. "Also the movement among the young men is unprecedented."—(*Alexander*).

16 For specially interesting conversions reference is made to the Works of God, (Kami no Miwaza) and a second series of similar incidents more recently published. The first series appeared in English and many thousands have been sold abroad. Dr. Haworth has been specially instrumental in spreading these in America and in lecturing there on the movement in general.

17 "At home (United States, England, etc.) the Taikyo Dendo has greatly revived the interest of Christian people in the evangelization of Japan and has supplied new courage for the evangelization of the world."—(*Imbrie*).

18 All means a heavy burden upon pastors for which they need our prayers. To follow up, conserve, deepen and extend the results is all-important. Mrs. Pierson's paper on this subject in the Japan Evangelist of April and May, 1901, deserves special mention. Y. P. S. C. E. should find a grand field of work and rich harvests; Sunday Schools too.

19 The Church has learned great lessons. Especially it "needs to realize more fully that it can undertake great things for God and expect great things from Him."—(*Hail*).

20 "Its (Taikyo Dendo) most valuable results are the new consecration of pastors and Christians, the new sense of the power of the simple Gospel, and the new assurance of victory."—(*S. L. Gulick*). Already a grand protracted effort during the coming National Exposition to be held in Osaka in 1903 is planned and well under way.

As planned for, the campaign was reopened in late spring of this year. Very good results have already been attained in Tokyo and Yokohama, and probably elsewhere. Several leaders in the work have given it as their conviction that a better, more staid and promising class is being reached in the inquiry rooms this year. While there is perhaps less sensation, the novelty having worn off, still we may look for perhaps even greater accessions to the churches this year. Several churches in Tokyo have had over a hundred inquirers each as the result of special meetings. In Yokohama the work has taken on a more promising phase even than last year, especially in the reclamation of members long lost to the church who are having their faith and life greatly requickened. This is a phase of the work that is very encouraging and calls for joyful recognition and strong emphasis.

4 The Japan Sabbath Alliance is still a fourth result of the Tokyo Missionary Conference. Its constitution has been formulated (see Japan Evangelist, June, 1901) and special efforts are to be made, to launch it in October. One of our reports says, " Can not some practical aggressive work be done on this line ? Surely we cannot hope for God's blessing while his laws are being so generally disregarded." In this Sabbath Alliance our Church ought to show special enthusiasm. Cannot our Council give efficient aid and encouragement to this Alliance? The work of the Alliance will prove a Sisyphean toil unless missionaries, pastors and churches enthusiastically coöperate. The July Japan Evangelist has a call for support from Christians,—membership fees 25 sen a year.

The angel of death has been in our midst laying his hand upon the helpmeet of one of our oldest colaborers. Heartfelt sympathies of the Council go out to Dr. Stout in his great bereavement.

Of those whom ill health has obliged to return from Japan, Dr.

Alexander easily heads the list; this is not the place however to form an estimate of the man or of his work, the less so as he really is not taken either out of mission work or out of contact with Japan; his work in Honolulu so far gives very cheering reports. Still he is greatly missed especially as founder and father of our West Japan Presbyterian Mission. The Kyoto report makes this clear.

This same Mission has also cause to regret the departure of Mr. and Mrs. Doughty, owing to the precarious state of Mrs. Doughty's health.

Miss Glenn and at latest accounts Miss Shaw are still others of this same Mission *who after a determined struggle not to succumb have to yield, at least for the time, and return to America.

Miss Wimbish too finds herself compelled to relinquish an earnest, self-sacrificing and fruitful work in order to find physical restoration elsewhere. Mr. and Mrs. Hudson too have felt obliged to return home.

To these and others perhaps similarly threatened, the Council and indeed the Church of Christ in Japan owes a debt of sympathy, and an appropriate acknowledgment might go far to soothe pains, trials and regrets at being obliged to lay down a service which when undertaken was hoped to be a life privilege.

The church building record of the year calls for note here. If every year should see a similar number built, there would be a good supply in a short time. That some of them depended on their own resources, at least in good part, is also an evidence of progress in the right direction. Herewith a list of those built or at least planned to be built soon:

    A. ERECTED:—　　　　　　B. IN PROSPECT:—
        Tokyo,　　　　　　　　　　　Nagoya.
            Daimachi.　　　　　　　　Toyohashi.
            Tsunohazu.　　　　　　　Meiji Gakuin, Tokyo.
            Meguro.　　　　　　　　　Ichibancho, Tokyo.
        Kyoto.　　　　　　　　　　　Takamatsu.†

* Another lady of this Mission Miss Nivling in becoming Mrs. Madeley, is lost to this Mission but fortunately adds her labors to a sister denomination.

† Our present meeting place is too crowded; so plans have been initiated for the erection of a suitable place of worship. A good lot has recently been bought and paid for, but this leaves us with very little money on hand for building. For this purpose the Christians have given about $250.00 (*yen*) during the past year.—(*Buchanan*).

Kiriu.
Okazaki.
Asahigawa,—also a parsonage.
Seto.
Sendai (perhaps the pleasantest church building in Japan).

Dr. Schneder writes:—In Sendai a large new church building was dedicated in October of last year. The building has helped to call attention to Christianity. Thirty-one persons have been baptized in the church since its dedication and there are many new inquirers. A good beginning has been made with the merchant class. The officials and other prominent people of Sendai city are friendly to the Christian cause. Last year many of the leading ladies of the city helped Mrs. Schneder in an enterprise to raise money for a church fence.

Mr. Myers writes thus:—As reported last year we have a new church building in Tokushima; and our advice to all who have dark inconvenient Kogisho's is,—Build as soon as you can. Put your woman's society to work, and tell all your friends about it. Then, if your ideas are not too big, it is astonishing how soon you will have enough. A comfortable convenient building is certainly a great help to the work in Japan as well as in America.

Mr. Price writes:—The increasing cost of land and building material makes the question of building suitable churches without giving them to the Japanese Christians and thus injuring the cause of selfsupport, a difficult one. Yet the need of proper buildings is becoming greater every year. Th eraising of building and loan funds to be loaned to weak churches without interest for a fixed term of years seems a possible solution of the question. Buildings we must have but how can we get them?

EDUCATIONAL WORK.

A. THEOLOGICAL SCHOOLS.

MEIJI GAKUIN, DR. IMBRIE:—"The work of the Theological Department of the Meiji Gakuin has gone on during the past year smoothly and without interruption; the relations between the teachers and the students have been most cordial; and it is hoped that good has been done.

The new students number eight; the largest accession in a single year for a considerable time. It is believe that this is the result of improved conditions in the Church; and that it is to be regarded as good reason for encouragement. The entire number of students now in attendance is thirteen.

Mr. Ibuka, in addition to the performance of his many duties connected with the Meiji Gakuin and the Church, found or made time to be one of the lecturers at the summer school for students both last summer and this and also for two evangelistic tours—one on the West coast and one in the Hokkaido. Mr. Kashiwai, (an instructor in the school), has made a translation of Nicoll's The Incarnate Saviour which has been published, and which has won praise for its excellence. He has also been working on a life of Drummond and planning for one of Bunyan. Mr. Kuwada, who graduated in the spring, is still stationed at Mito, where he works in connection with the Board of Home Missions of the Church, and where he is well reported of.

But the event for which the year will especially be remembered is the active participation of the Southern Presbyterians in the work of the school. The mission of that Church is represented by the Rev. S. P. Fulton who removed to Tokyo in November to the great pleasure of all. Since then he has done his full share of work in the school, and has been in constant demand for the exercise of his gifts among the churches.

It remains only to express the hope that the day may not be far distant when the Mission of the Reformed Church will once more be represented among the teachers in the school, a hope that may be realized in Mr. Oltmans' coming after his return from furlough. Besides taking part in the instruction of the students for the future ministry of the Church, such a one will find a wide field for evangelistic work in Tokyo and the surrounding country."

STATISTICS:
- Students . . . 13
- Graduates . . 2

Teachers:
- Foreigners 2
- Japanese 3

The TOHOKU GAKUIN, (*Sendai Theo. Dep.*) reports 11 theological students, 7 of whom were graduated at the close of the school year. All graduated, (one a member of the Kumiai Church) are already engaged in direct evangelistic work.

STATISTICS:
- Students 11
- Graduates 7

Teachers:
- Foreigners . . . . . . 3?
- Japanese . . . . . . 5?

The Nagasaki Theological Department is reported as suspended.

There is one subject strongly emphasized by a number of reports, viz. the lack of Japanese evangelists. Mr. Peeke: "We have not the force to do anything for them" (the rural classes).

MR. PIETERS:—(At the close of his report), "Further than this I do not know that I have anything to say unless it be to reaffirm the necessity of our laboring actively and earnestly in prayer and doctrine that young men may be led to devote themselves to the ministry. The other day I was talking with a minister of the Nihon Kirisuto Kyokwai on the matter of getting two bright young men in the Koto Gakko here to become preachers. He said with an incredulous smile: 'There is no hope of that. Those fellows are too bright, their prospects of success in life are too good to expect them to do such a thing.' I am afraid this spirit prevails only too largely. It is time for us to make this a special object of prayer and endeavor."

Mr. OLTMANS:—"What stares us in the face at present and fills us more or less with fear is the serious depletion and consequent inadequacy of the number of our Japanese evangelists. In our field we can only supply two of our outstations with a resident evangelist and the prospects are a decrease in number without any candidates in theological training,—this at a time when so many gospel doors stand wide open seems specially regrettable. As a Council of Missions we should bear this matter seriously on our hearts and also see if there is not something we can and ought to do in the way of devising means for supplying this serious defect."

Mr. PRICE:—"After a busy year (one of the) three things most needed seems to be more workers in the harvest field. I should like to see some plan proposed by which worthy Japanese wishing to enter the ministry could do so even though their knowledge of English be very limited."

Mr. W. C. BUCHANAN:—Speaking of the few workers for Sanuki, continues,—" No doubt a dearth of workers is experienced elsewhere, but we sincerely hope that there are no other places as badly off in this respect as Sanuki. It may not be out of place to mention just here that several of our best men have felt the great call for more workers and their obligations toward Christ to heed that call. But the requirement for English in the Theological Department of the Meiji Gakuin effectually bars the doors of that institution to them and will possibly keep them forever out of the ministry. Let me venture the hope that the day in not far distant when the Missions controlling the Meiji Gakuin will establish a theological curriculum in the vernacular and thus give practical expression to the belief that doubtless lies it the heart of every missionary,—that a man who knows nothing whatever of English, may be called to preach the gospel."

Mr. S. P. FULTON:—"On account of the lack of workers the country places have been more or less abandoned."

MR. AYRES:—" We have been short of helpers. We had money for one more last year than we had men and have now two organized churches without regular preaching and another church where the preacher is not at all sufficient for the importance of the place. We are anxiously looking for a man or two."

Mr. BALLAGH:—"O, for hundred fold more laborers and for a vast increase of faith in the proclamation of the gospel!"

Dr. THOMPSON:—"From lack of qualified preachers and the means to support them in their work, (a number of) places have all been left to take care of themselves."

Mr. MILLER, H. K.:—"We are confronted with difficulties in manning our work."

Thus we have the cry for helpers in the great harvest field from South to North. Surely while in this year of the Forward Movement we lift up our eyes and look on the fields and see them already white to harvest, we ought, since laborers are so few, to heed Jesus' call, "Pray ye therefore the Lord of the harvest that he thrust forth laborers into his harvest."

Amid all this plaint we have one voice of hope from the far North: "There are four new candidates for the ministry in our field, two in the Mombetsu region and two in Asahigawa."

Ought not all our educational and evangelistic workers to make very special efforts to bring this great theme prominently in all its dimensions before those for whom they labor? and ought we not to interest the Japanese ministry in this theme?

B. BIBLE WOMEN'S SCHOOLS.

SEISHO GAKKWAN, TOKYO, PRESBYTERIAN (NORTH).

STATISTICS:
    Pupils . . . 15
    Graduates . . . 2
Teachers:
    Foreigners 2
    Japanese 2

MRS. MACNAIR, who has complete charge in the absence of Miss West in the United States this year, reports as follows:—

"The Training School for Bible-women has passed another satisfactory year of work. Fifteen students have been in attendance and two have been graduated. We regret to report the loss of one student by death from quick consumption in one of the city hospitals. She passed away quietly after three weeks of extreme weakness, during which her faith never wavered.

Four Bible-women have been employed, one in the town of Kisarazu in Kazusa, one in hospital and general work in Tokyo, another in connection with one of the largest of the city churches, and a fourth since the autumn of last year in Shinagawa.

In this department of our work death has also entered and claimed one of our most faithful workers. In August of last year Mrs. Oka, after several weeks of illness in her home in the Shinagawa school building, was taken to the University hospital where she died in a few hours. She was one of whom it may truly be said "faithful unto death," and we may confidently believe that the crown of life is her reward."

WOMANS UNION MISSION, 212 BLUFF YOKOHAMA.

Pupils in training	26
Bible Women in the work	36

MISS CROSBY:—"The record of the year in the evangelistic department of our work has been an encouraging one. The corps of Bible readers numbers sixty-two, comprising women of various ages. Of these twenty-six of the younger members are still in the training school, pursuing the regular four years' course of study. Some of the others are engaged in daily house-to-house visitation in Yokohama and vicinity, or in the out-stations, while others, living in their homes, do the same work in their own villages. Interesting reports come in from time to time from these workers, and there have been a number of conversions and baptisms.

During the past few months the work at an outstation in Boshiu has been especially encouraging. The people gather in large numbers eager to hear the truth, several have received baptism, and there are many earnest inquirers. There is also a crowded Sunday School conducted by the two faithful Bible women who have been stationed there during the winter. We are praying that many souls may be gathered in from this field which seems to be "white already to harvest."

One memorable event of the year was the visit of our Secretary, Miss Doremus, who was with us in April. No officer of our Society since its organization in 1860, has ever before visited its work in the East. The coming of Miss Doremus, was therefore an occurrence of no small moment to us, as well as to all our stations in India and China. Her visit was a great stimulus and inspiration to us all, our only regret being that it was so very short.

Acknowledging with sincere gratitude the many blessings of the past, we are entering upon the new year with fresh hope and courage, humbly depending upon our Heavenly Father to grant us all needed grace and strength for its duties as they come to us day by day."

Both Ferris Seminary and Sturges Seminary have departments for training Bible women, but the numbers in attendance are as yet very small. Miyagi Jogakko also trains Bible women.

B. Bible Schools for Evangelists.

Mr. Oltmans to whom we have been looking for the Saga Bible School's doings reports that this year it was postponed till the coming autumn, when the Epistle to the Romans is to be the special theme.

The Hokkaido Conference approaches this line of work. It is to be held this August again.

At Nagaoka a session of a like nature was held under the auspices of the German Reformed Mission.

Workers' conferences have been held in connection with the Synod, also in Sendai and other places.

C. Boys Boarding Schools.

Meiji Gakuin Academic Department.

The year has been more than usually prosperous. The number enrolled in September, reached 170, while in April of this year it reached nearly 200; still a number owing to irregular attendance and other reasons have dropped from the roll so that about 170 represented the attendance in June. Many applications for the highest class were refused during the year partly because of the size of the class and partly because students coming only for a few months to get a diploma are in the main an undesirable element, and moreover very little influence of a Christian order can be exercised in so short a time over such material. A few students are in the advanced course; an effort is made to develop this course, especially as special privileges for this course too have been received from the government. To gain this end the course had to be extended to 3 years. No doubt, especially if the privileges in the ordinary course be fully recovered again, this course too will fill up in time, especially when the Normal School privileges too are fully obtained.

The work goes on steadily. Religiously the school has been greatly blessed. A year ago more than 40 expressed their desire to become Christians; 32 of these were then received into Church membership. We may attribute this partly no doubt to daily religious instruction in the course and to the general religious atmosphere of the institution. During Mr. Mott's work in October, 9 more declared for Christ while since then several more have been actively interested. These with others are afforded regular instruction in experimental religion by Pres. Ibuka outside of the course so as to get clearer ideas on the essentials of Christianity. Attendance at prayer meetings and Sunday services has also increased. In all directions there is a hopeful atmosphere. Plans are in progress for the building of a new Chapel with funds realized from a building donated by a member of this Council.

A large proportion of the teachers are Christian, and as rapidly as qualified Christian teachers can be secured they are accepted for vacancies.

STATISTICS:

Foreign teachers	2
Japanese „	10
Pupils	170
Graduates	27
Converts	45
Christians	80

TOHOKU GAKUIN, SENDAI.

DR. SCHNEDER writes:—"The Tohoku Gakuin has had a fairly prosperous year. The average number of students during the year ending with March was 129. The number baptized during the year was 29, a result which was hastened by the visit of Mr. John R. Mott last fall. The number of Christians at the end of the school year was 51 out of a total of 104. Besides Bible study in the school, there is a weekly prayer-meeting in the dormitories, one Bible class on Saturday evening and another on Sunday morning, in addition to the church services, all of which are well attended by the students. At the end of the school year there were four graduates from the general course. Last January the school obtained the recognition which gives it postponement of military conscription. This has had the effect of largely increasing the number of applicants at the beginning of the new term, 184 students applying for entrance this spring, of whom owing to want of room only 75 could be admitted. Four missionaries give part of their time to the school."

Mr. Noss adds:—" Dr. Schneder's administration of Tohoku Gakuin, aided by Dr. Sasao and Professor Kajiwara, has been a great success. He had many misgivings about taking Mr. Oshikawa's place as president of the school, but he is unquestionably the best man for the place and our Japanese brethren have the grace to recognize the fact. The school is in better condition than it has been for years. The attendance at chapel and the demeanor of the students there is especially gratifying."

STATISTICS:
  Pupils 129
  Christians . . . 51
  Converts 29
TEACHERS:
  Foreigners . . . 4
  Japanese 13

STEELE COLLEGE, NAGASAKI.

STATISTICS:
  Pupils . 100
TEACHERS:
  Foreign 2
  Japanese 10

DR. STOUT:—"I wish I had something interesting to tell you about the school, but *domo* I have not. This is not because conditions have been unfavorable or that no results have been accomplished, but because everything has gone on in the even tenor of its way, there having been not even a semblance of a disturbance nor any remarkable developments, and because I am lacking in the imagination requisite to the working out of an interesting report under such circumstances. Even Taikyo Dendo, in which the Y. M. C. A. members took an active part, and the visits of Mr. Mott and Dr. Torrey, whose addresses were well received and whose appeals met with considerable response, seem to have made little or no permanent impression. However, I am happy to say that there has never been a more healthy moral tone in the institution, not a more general and interested attendance upon the ordinary means of grace, both in the school and in the church, than has prevailed for a considerable time and still continues. From this it seems to me there is reason to hope that there are influences at work that are bound to tell in happy results, perhaps in the near future."

D. Girls Boarding Schools.

Ferris Seminary.

Mr. Booth:—"Ferris Seminary, was established in 1875, by the Board of Foreign Missions of the Reformed Church in America.

It has three departments. The preparatory of three years; the grammar department of four years; and the Bible course of two years. The pupils are given daily instruction in the Bible in all the departments, daily systematic physical exercise under a competent teacher, instruction in sewing twice each week, flower-arrangement, *chinoyu* and etiquette to those who desire these accomplishments, instruction in vocal music, lessons on the organ to those who have the Bible course in view, and to others who pay the fees charged for them, also piano lessons to those who desire and pay for them.

The studies of the preparatory department are chiefly Japanese language, reading and writing, geography, arithmetic, with one exercise a day in colloquial English.

The studies of the grammar course are chiefly a drill in the Japanese and English languages, universal geography, arithmetic, history, elementary physics, botany, physiology, and free hand drawing. The Bible course consists of sacred history, introduction to the books of the

Old and New Testaments, sacred geography, biographical study of the chief characters in the Old and New Testaments, 'the coming Messiah (*a*) in type, (*b*) in predictions, (*c*) in the Advent, God's revelation of Himself to man, or God seeking to make Himself known to man, and man's relation to God in worship, with practical studies in God's methods in training workers.

One pupil has completed this course and is giving excellent satisfaction as a Christian worker.

For about eight years the school had a higher department, which was practically a normal course, as we were able, by means of it, to train our own teachers. But six years ago, through a misapprehension arising, perhaps from a fear that the education afforded was relatively too high, this course was discontinued. That unfortunate step has been marked by two disastrous consequences. One is that we no longer have the class of Christian teachers we formerly had. There being no graduates from the higher course, we are obliged to get what teachers we can. Christian teachers are difficult to find, and we must pay from twenty-five to fifty yen a month instead of from fifteen to thirty. The other is that pupils prefer to enter a school having a higher course, and either pass us by, or if they come, many, finding that the higher course is not likely to materialize, leave us after a year or two, and enter some other school where there is a higher course. It is my conviction that mission schools must pay more attention to their methods, and not only provide facilities to do better quality of work, than some of them are doing, but must also attain a higher grade than that of the present grade of the Ferris Seminary, or they will forfeit the patronage of the self-respecting and self-supporting Japanese.

To illustrate what I mean, I can do no better than refer to facts in relation to the class entering year before last. It numbered eighteen; at the close of the first year it was augmented by four other pupils entering it from the preparatory department, two of whom were on scholarships, two other members of the class being already on scholarships, making four assisted pupils; this made 22 at the beginning of the second year. At the close of the second year it numbered fifteen. It now numbers at the beginning of the third year four pupils, all of whom are on scholarships, which means that they have free tuition and board.

This means simply that we are adjudged competent to do a year or two of drill-work in the beginning of the acquisition of the English language, but for the rest, they will have none of it, unless there are better inducements offered.

The teachers are Rev. and Mrs. Booth in charge, Miss A. de F. Thompson, who returned from America in September, Miss Julia Moulton, Miss Harriet J. Wyckoff, who taught in the school in the early part of the year, and in January and February during Miss Thompson's illness, six Japanese teachers, a matron, and three others who taught special branches. Miss Wyckoff is to give her time hereafter to the Bible course pupils. There were ninety-six enrolled during the year in all departments, distributed as follows:—

Bible course	3
Grammar course	68
Preparatory	25
Total	96

At present there are eighty-two as follows.—

Bible course	2
Grammar course	62
Preparatory	18
Total	82

One less than was reported a year ago.

There were, four graduates, one from the Bible course and three from the grammar department.

Fifty-three are Christians. Ten were baptized during the year, one more confessed her faith, having been baptized in childhood, one other is a candidate for baptism.

The Christian pupils took a deep and intelligent interest in Taikyo Dendo. Some of them sang at the church door to attract the attention of passers-by, others stood at the gate, and invited people in.

Concluding this report of the school, I would like to remark that the conditions in this country, and the opportunities for succesful work for mission girls schools were never better, but the schools are unable to meet the conditions or to enbrace the opportunities offered; because of their inadequate equipment, and obsolete methods, non-Christian schools are out-stripping us. And the young womanhood of Japan is consequently being filled with the "husks" of intellectualism. Here is a fact that may very materially retard the evangelization of Japan. Would it not, therefore, be good policy for the Council to make suitable representations to the responsible parties and urge upon them the necessity of doing something to make our girls schools more effective. The tentative measures of pioneer days are now useless. Why should we continue sentimental in this branch of the work, when the conditions demand our meeting them intelligently, conscientiously, and enthusiastically."

WOMAN'S UNION MISSION, 212 BLUFF YOKOHAMA.

STATISTICS:

Pupils	63
Graduates	5
Christians	37
United with church during the year	15
Foreign teachers	3?
Japanese teachers	11

MISS CROSBY:—"In many respects the past year has been one of marked blessing to our school. There has been a gradual increase in the number of pupils, and the corps of missionaries has been happily reinforced by the arrival early in the winter, of Miss Clara D. Loomis. Several improvements in text-books and methods of instruction have been introduced, and more attention has been given to physical culture.

There is daily Bible work in all the classes. Some of Dr. Torrey's excellent books, such as the "Doctrine of Man," the "Doctrine of the Holy Spirit," &c. have furnished pleasant and profitable helps in the Scripture lessons of the Seniors. The Juniors have been studying the Old Testament and are now intensely interested in Isaiah read in the light of history. A carefully planned course in the Gospels has been arranged for the lower classes and the pupils have become so familiar with this portion of God's word that every incident, miracle, and parable can be readily located by them. A summary of every chapter in each gospel is memorized, and this has proved a most satisfactory method with the younger girls. Eight conversions were the result of the lessons on the twenty-fourth of Matthew, and there were other pupils baptized at different times, making fifteen baptisms in all during the year. At the commencement a class of eight graduated. Of these, five remain to take up the postgraduate course and as pupil teachers; one is taking a special course of study in Tokyo; one is planning to enter the evangelistic department in the autumn, and the other one has returned to her home.

The school has its own literary society and W. C. T. U. which hold their regular meetings and carry on their business with becoming dignity through their properly appointed officers. But older than either of these, though quite as vigorous, is the school Missionary Society which was organized in 1875. This society carries on and supports three mission S. schools with a membership of over one hundred, providing the funds necessary for rent of rooms, &c., besides always giving the children a good Christmas treat. They also contribute to two orphanages, and five of the members are teachers in the church Sunday school.

Joshi Gakuin, Tokyo.

STATISTICS:

No. of pupils . .	203
Boarders . . .	102
Christians . .	60
United with church	9
Teachers:	
Foreign ladies .	5
Japanese teachers . .	12

MISS MILLIKEN:—"At the Joshi Gakuin the year has been one of quiet prosperity. The corps of Japanese teachers is more than usually efficient and among the pupils the feeling of emulation caused by the opening of several new schools, notably the "Girls University" and Miss Tsuda's school, has lent a new impetus to study.

Among the foreign teachers there have been a number of changes. Miss Helena Wyckoff, daughter of Dr. Wyckoff of the Meiji Gakuin, is a most welcome addition to the faculty. She began work in September. Miss Ballagh left on furlough in October and Miss Gardner in April. The latter had hoped to remain until a new missionary arrived from America but the state of her health made immediate departure imperative. The Misses Thompson have continued their valued services and during the spring term, Miss MacAdam of the American Episcopal Mission, has kindly given three mornings a week. Thus it has been possible, notwithstanding the reduced force, to keep up the regular class-work.

As to the number of pupils the limit of those who can be accommodated to advantage has been reached. Once more, as in the '80's, we are having to refuse applicants. The aim now set before us is increasing efficiency. At the opening of the spring term there were 203 in attendance, 102 of whom were boarders. The character of the new pupils is of a kind particularly desirable, some being graduates from other mission schools, some the daughters of our own "old girls," a few the children of ministers of our own Church, who always claim a warm welcome, and many from families just around us in Bancho.

Among the day-pupils an earnest interest in the daily Bible lessons, has been manifest. A number of them asked for special instruction, with opportunity to ask questions, on Sunday afternoons. Miss Mitani gave them two hours each Sunday for a number of weeks and now the members of this class have all commenced regular attendance upon church services.

As a result of the Taikyō Dendō movement last year closed with almost all the older girls Christians. The nine baptisms this year have been from among the younger girls. Last year over 50 professed conversion; several more of these are preparing to unite with the church. There are others, who hope they are Christians, patiently waiting for permission from their homes to make public profession of their faith.

The older girls have lent assistance as teachers or organists in ten Sunday-schools. The one in which the deepest interest has centred is a school for very poor children in Shinano Machi. That the pupils there are at least as enthusiastic as the teachers would seem to be indicated by the fact that they gather a full hour before the time for opening. The slender attendance on rainy days only means that those who do not come are without umbrellas. One little pupil who was ill for months still counted Sunday the best day in the week because it brought him a visit from his teacher. To him heavenly things grew real and bright as his little body wasted away and he passed so joyously to the heavenly home that those who had taught him to say "Our

Father" felt that no other joy could be more precious than ministering to such "little ones."

The four girls who graduated in March all expressed a wish to do some form of Christian work. One has gone to the Naniwa Jo Gakko in Osaka, one to a Christian kindergarten in Nagano, one to do evangelistic work in Toyohashi and one is to go this summer to Sapporo, as assistant to Miss Daughaday.

Visits made in the homes of present and former pupils have been so cordially received as to make us wish many more could be paid. Everything seems to indicate that next year will present more openings than we have had for a decade. With the increased force of workers which we hope for we may be able to lengthen the cords and strengthen the stakes. This bright outlook, as well as present blessing, makes it meet that we close the year in the spirit of gratitude."

Turning to the three girls' schools of the West Japan Presbyterian Mission, Mr. Dunlop, as member of a committee appointed in the autumn of 1901 to investigate and report on girls' schools to the Mission, gives the result of that work as follows:—

"It was the great and increasing difficulties under which our school work has labored for the past year or two that led to the Mission's decision to take stock of its school interests, find out just where we stand, and whether there is any possibility of a better adjustment, looking as well to better work as to a still finer economy in the management of our schools. The difficulties have been short funds, competition with newly opened government schools, some official jealousy and interference in places, and, more than any thing else, the breakdowns among missionary ladies and the scarcity of Japanese teachers. It has been hard to keep up a Japanese staff, and harder still to keep up a missionary staff for the schools. The Mission's committee set out to see if haply, when our force of ladies is so run down, some of this arduous school work may not well be given up, or whether some of the energies of our lady missionaries may not well be directed into purely evangelistic channels, less trying perhaps to the physical constitution. The conclusion of the committee and of the Mission was like that of the hard pressed father and mother who were asked to give up one of their numerous children in adoption to a wealthy relative. They could part with none of them, so precious did each appear.

Never before did school work for girls appear so valuable or so desirable. Three facts that especially impressed the committee were these: 1 That so far as our schools, at any rate are concerned, there is no propriety in speaking of school work and evangelistic work as though the two were in contrast to each other. The fact is, our school work is evangelistic work, and very successful and valuable evangelistic work at that. 2 That the higher the grade of the work for girls, the more valuable it appeared. It is a mistake and a great pity to let the pupils go before they have attained the years and development and strength of character that will ensure their holding fast that which is the best in the education given them. 3 That by far the best work is done among boarding pupils.

The principal recommendation of the committee was one looking to closer contact between the Mission and its schools; that the schools be treated more as schools of the Mission rather than local institutions under the station or under an individual or individuals in the station. A Mission Committee on Education was appointed to have a general supervision over all the school work of the Mission. Provision was made also for bringing the three (3) girls' schools of the Mission more into uniformity as regards years of study and curricula."

To an interested onlooker a few remarks may be allowed here:—

Would it not be advisable to thoroughly organize all these schools and perhaps the Nagoya Kinjo Jo-Gakko, together with the C. P. Wilmina Girls School in Osaka, (all in central Japan), into a thorough system, the details of which can neither be presented or argued here, among the main objects however being the following:—

1 Securing economy of effort and expenditure together with a maximum of result in work accomplished, grade of work attained and number of students reached.

2 A system which implies that one school, centrally located should be a center offering advanced opportunities to which others shall become feeders. In other words, locate one well equipped high school including lower department in Osaka and plan that all the other schools aim to send their best to it. This would imply that Naniwa and Wilmina Girls Schools either become one (the ideal plan) or at least that one of these limit itself strictly to primary grade work, while the other with an adequate corps of teachers, foreign and Japanese, and otherwise equipped to

cope with the splendidly equipped government girls schools of Osaka, and with Kobe College too, rise to a really commanding position among girls schools in this country. Even leaving Kobe College out of que tion (which can hardly be done unless we are quite ready that all our girls schools shall become in a very real sense feeders to it), is it not apparent that those two well equipped and high grade government girls schools in Osaka, and possibly also soon positive government requirements for all girls schools in Osaka, will force our schools to the wall in a very discomforting sense of that term?

3 We are one Church, one Council, union is in the air even between all Protestant bodies, things are moving forward to a goal, and why should we in our own peculiar work as foreign missions and missionaries be ultra conservative or even reactionary where school work is concerned?

4 We shall be met by the retort, "Physician, heal thyself." Be it so. Let Tokyo and Yokohama also take the cue. Perhaps the argument applies there too. We only state that the Joshi Gakuin has from different sources won encomiums for doing work in female education second to none in the country, and that one (unfortunately in the main an impossible) argument of the West Japan Mission has been to make its schools feeders to the Joshi Gakuin. Where distance and other things like nearer institutions come into play, a pretty theory cannot always bend facts to suit it.

NANIWA JOGAKKO, OSAKA, W. J. PRESBYTERIAN (NORTH).

STATISTICS:
    Pupils enrolled . . 80
    Christians 30
    United with church during the year . 5
    Foreign teachers 2
    Japanese teachers 9

Miss GARVIN:—"Whole course of study, 6 years; all but the lowest year are above Koto Sho Gakko (Higher Primary School) grade; graduates 4, post graduates 2.

There is in the school a large C. E. society (60 members) carried on successfully by the students. Eleven students engaged in S. S. work."

HOKURIKU JOGAKKO KANAZAWA, W. J. PRESBYTERIAN (NORTH).

STATISTICS:
- Pupils . . 40
- Christians . . 21
- United with church . 5

Teachers:
- Foreign ladies 3
- Japanese . . . . ?

MISS SHAW:—"This school has now entered upon its eighteenth school-year, as seventeen years of work closed March 25th.

There are good prospects for prosperity. We have had sixty-two pupils enrolled since the report of last year was written.

We lost six from removals, marriages &c., and graduated five in March; so we closed school with a much smaller number than we had had for some years. But we gained twenty-three new pupils, which is the largest number we have ever had enter at the beginning of any term, most able to enter our first year of the regular course in Japanese, though two years behind in English. This has greatly encouraged the teachers and older pupils.

Last July our principal for eight years, resigned his position and went elsewhere. So, from August till April I was in the interesting business of "hunting a man." After many failures at the last one gentleman said he would like to come and could come! He has thus far proved very satisfactory. We have an excellent corps of teachers, and with as many pupils as we ever had, or nearly so, we are much encouraged in the work.

Last June five of our girls were baptised. Some have given evidences of a change of heart since. There have been twenty-two baptised Christians in the school during the year and six more whom we felt were believers. All the Christian work, societies and benevolencies have been kept up to their usual standard. This spring the C. E. Society sent a delegate to the Osaka Convention. Their banner took third prize, which was not bad, considering that there were over forty of them.

Last September Miss Glenn returned to the school and tried bravely to, 'do her share,' as she put it, but disease would not yield to treatment. Though she seemed much better through the Fall and early winter she was not well, and this spring she grew so much worse that it was decided that she must return to the United States as soon as possible.

God shows his blessing and help constantly, even though so many changes and draw-backs do come. So we trust him for all the future has in store." Since the above was written, Miss Shaw too has been obliged by ill health to return to America.

KOJO JO GAKUIN, W. J. PRESBYTERIAN (NORTH) YAMAGUCHI.

STATISTICS:

Pupils	36
Graduates	2
Church members	5
Converts	3

Teachers:

Foreign	1
Japanese	8

MISS BIGELOW: — "Yamaguchi people are very conservative. When interest in the education of girls was at its height in Tokyo more than ten years ago, Yamaguchi's pulse does not seem to have fluttered. But at last there is universal movement in the ken.

The Koto Jo Gakko here is full, and a few of the more liberal who can endure the thought of their daughters learning Christianity, have sent them to us. We have more pupils than ever before. Thirty-six have been enrolled this spring and we cannot well accommodate many more. As more than half of these are new pupils, the number of Christians in the school is small. There are five church members, and several are candidates for baptism.

Of the teachers, five are Christians. Three who only come for two hours a week are not.

Two pupils were graduated in April. They were both Christians and both have gone into kindergarten work.

We find it very hard to keep girls until they graduate. In the vicissitudes of this school-year our two upper classes have completely vanished."

Kinjo Jogakko, S. Presbyterian, Nagoya.

Statistics:

Pupils	62
Graduates	?
Christians	33
Converts	12

Teachers:

Foreign	2
Japanese	?

Miss Houston:—"The Kinjo Jogakko has made no special history this year; 62 pupils have been enrolled. Of this number thirty-three are Christians, twelve having been baptized during the year. Nearly all the others are earnestly inquiring. The prospects for the school both as regards numbers, and what is more important development of Christian life and character were never better. The school had a good commencement."

Wilmina Girls School, Cumberland Presbyterian, Osaka.

Miss Morgan:—"The year ending in March was very encouraging. The school has been growing and doing good work. Although we began the school eighteen years ago, with the rise and growth of the reaction against girls schools, our patronage so decreased that we practically began anew in January 1900; we feel much encouraged over our steady growth since then. The general sentiment about higher education for girls and the ambition and work of the girls themselves, are very encouraging, though there is much room for improvement yet along these lines. But there is already a sense of need and a desire for knowledge. The interest in the Bible classes is very good indeed, but that depends upon the teacher's power much more than the ordinary studies do; however when an interest is seen we know it is not founded upon parents' choice or popular sentiment as to what a girl should study.

STATISTICS:

Total enrollment	70
Average attendance.	46
Boarding pupils	20
Day pupils	26
Christian pupils	28
Baptisms	2
Missionaries connected with school	2
Native teachers	6

Grade of School—Higher Primary through High-School.

We have not had the highest class since the new opening and so have no graduates to report.

I have work with one of our churches in Osaka, holding women's meetings, teaching the women's Bible class on Sundays, superintending the children's Sunday School where our Christian pupils are trained to teach, etc. I feel we have much room for thankfulness and hope from the recent awakening to new life and privileges and duty we have seen in the church and for what we will continue to see along the same lines."

STURGES SEMINARY, R. C. A. (DUTCH) NAGASAKI.

STATISTICS:

No. of pupils	55
„ „ Christians in Steele Academy and Sturges Seminary	21
Foreign teachers	2
Japanese lady teachers	5
„ men teachers (in Sturges Seminary and Steele Academy)	11

MISS COUCH :—" I would report an increased religious interest during the latter part of our school-year. This seemed largely brought about through the visit of Mr. Torrey.

Although we have had no additions to the church from among our girls, five have joined over Christian Endeavor Society as associate members. The interest in this society as well as in that of the King's Daughters seems to be well-sustained.

Since last September one elderly Christian woman has been receiving special Bible instruction in connection with the school.

Last autumn I found it possible to spend three weeks touring in the Kagoshima district. The meetings for women and children were nearly all well attended. This spring I have made two brief visits to Sasebo where there is a flourishing woman's society."

MIYAGI JOGAKKO SENDAI, R. C. U. S. A. (GERMAN.)

STATISTICS:

Pupils	70
Graduates	8
Converts	?
Foreign teachers	3
Japanese ,,	10

MISS POWELL:—"In September Miss Weidner and I were joined by Miss B. Catherine Pifer.

Our work on the whole has been encouraging.

On March 8th our school building with most of its contents was destroyed by fire. No lives were lost, but some of the teachers and pupils lost all or part of their personal belongings. We have rented a Japanese building in which we are now carrying on our school work. We are of course laboring under difficulties as the buildings are not adequate in size or kind. But we hope to have larger and better equipped buildings in the near future. In spite of this disaster the opening of the spring term was very encouraging. Forty-seven new students were admitted, of whom but two are Christians. On account of our limited quarters we were compelled to refuse many applications for admission. Of these new girls eight are boarders. The others live in their homes or with friends in Sendai.

We have in the preparatory course sixteen, in the regular course eighty-five, in all one hundred and one girls, of whom forty are boarders. Besides these, the eight girls who graduated this year are doing some post-graduate work.

We have with us twenty-five of our graduates as helpers, tutors, teachers and Bible women. Nine of our school girls are doing work in the various Sunday schools.

During the year two girls have become Christians. A deep interest is being shown by others, and we hope that they too ere long will join the Christian ranks. Girls who at first were disposed to make light of Bible study are becoming earnest students of the Scriptures and regular attendants of our Sunday schools.

We hope another year to report that we are in our own new buildings.

We are looking forward to the return of Miss Zurfluh in August."

HOKUSEI JOGAKKO SAPPORO, E. J. PRESBYTERIAN (NORTH.)

STATISTICS:

Total number of pupils . . .	123
Average attendance . . .	96
Church members	33
United with church during the year	12
Foreign lady teachers . . .	2
Japanese ,, ,,	5
,, men ,,	4

MISS SMITH :—

1 "Many favorable results from Taikyo Dendo : Increase of church attendance and church membership, closer union of denominations and more general study of Christianity.

2 While there are but thirty-three church members, there are several more Christians; some whose parents will not consent to baptism but who take part in all our religious services and work. Seven are teachers in our two Sunday-schools in which there are about two hundred pupils. One is the home school, the other the church school. The former is in charge of Miss Wells and the latter in that of one of the church people. The younger Christian girls gather the children for the Sunday-schools. Our King's Daughters and Helping-Hands Societies in the school have, by work and collection, raised *yen* 37.35 but school duties prevent much work in this line.

3 Bible women,—one regular, one who travels and holds meetings and visits from house to house and works in connection with the church, and a younger one whom I have had the past year to send to special cases or for special service ; two have had the salary of but one. When going on trips myself I have met with much encouragement from well attended meetings.

Finally, we are planning for new school buildings for the procuring of which, the property is being turned over to the Mission."

SEISHU JOGAKKO OTARU, E. J. PRESBYTERIAN (NORTH.)

This is not a boarding school, but otherwise does work like the above.

STATISTICS:
    Pupils 45
    Christians. 4

A kindergarten is connected with it in which are 22 children (boys). Miss Rose, the missionary in charge being absent in the U. S. no full report has been obtained.

E. DAY (OR PRIMARY SCHOOLS).

(These seem to be mostly confined to the Northern Presbyterian Missions E. and W.)

KEIMO, NOS. 1 AND 2, TOKYO, PRESBYTERIAN NORTH.

MRS. MCCAULEY:—"These two primary schools, Keimo No. 1 and Keimo No. 2, are situated in Tsukiji and Shiba, Tokyo. 1 *Tsukiji school*, Keimo No. 1, has an average attendance of 80. Number of boys, 38, girls 54, total enrolled 92, one death. Of the children who have left the school, the report is as follows, 10 are servants in houses, 10, are employed in making hairpins, cigar boxes, and match boxes. The school represents the following occupations: 23, children of jinriki men, 20, boatmen, 5, tobacco shop keepers, 5, blacksmiths, 3, coal dealers, 3, vegetable dealers, 2, brick makers, 3, tailors, 2, stone cutters, 2, furniture dealers, 2, fish dealers, 2, traveling restaurants 1, wine and sake shop, 1, dyer, 1, bean shop, 1, old clothes dealer, 1, house painter, 1, baker, 1, sugar store, 1, cabinet maker, 1, box maker, 1, shinto priest, 2, from Miss Youngman. The majority of the children, come from the boatmen, and jinriki men; hence the income from tuition is meager. Every family has been visited during the year; also during the Taikyo Dendo movement they were especially visited and invited to meetings. One of the teachers, not a Christian, when first employed, became so during year, and an active worker in the Taikyo Dendo movement. During the year, the outside children brought in as visitors to S. S. 253 in all, but they did not attend regularly. With the money collected in the S. school which is under Mrs. Thompson's oversight, a new S. school has been opened in Odawara-cho, taught by the teachers of Keimo No. 1, with an average of forty pupils. Two boys who finished the course last year have been baptized in Shinsakae Church. One of our little girls, a child of eleven, from a family of the direst poverty, was a child of striking beauty, which became a snare. The parents were offered help, if they would in exchange give this beautiful daughter to be trained for a singing girl. She sang the beautiful songs of salvation, and they remained in her soul. And fine clothes and dainty food could not blind her eyes to the impurity she saw in her new life. The teaching she had received lived in her heart, and she cried and wept till they let her go to see her parents. See begged and implored them not to send her back to that sinful life. She would do anything however hard, to help them. They relented. She again came to school and after a little while she got a place to work so that she may help others and live a pure life as well.

A Shinto priest sent his son just on trial at Christmas time; the boy received a Bible and told his father that the Bible taught that the Creator was much greater than the thing created; the father began reading the Bible, and the result is that the priest has sent three more children from his diocese to us.

2. *Shiba School, Keimo No. 2.*

The whole number enrolled during the year	206
Number received during the year . .	95
Number left during the year	86
Average attendance during the year. . .	120

Of these ten are orphans from Mita, Tokyo. *One girl* graduated from Koto department, became a Christian and was baptized in Shiba Church during Taikyo Dendo movement. 18 finished the usual course, 15 of these being girls, and 3 boys. 5 of the eighteen come from Christian homes. During the year 2 boys, and 2 girls and 1 graduate united with the church, making 5 in all from the school within the year. 10 of the parents have been led by the children to come to church and two of these are now among the inquirers asking for baptism; 1 was baptized on his dying bed. Many trades and occupations are represented in the school. Small merchants, are in the majority; next come jinrikishamen, coachmen, wood and coal dealers; only one comes from the home of an official. Ten Christian homes are represented in the school, not 8% of the school. Five teachers are employed, 2 men and three women, all Christians.

Christian Work.

One hour a day is given to Bible study and catechism on the New Testament and the Old Testament, a midweekly prayermeeting, an hour a week to singing hymns, a teachers' noon prayermeeting on Saturday at the close of the week's work, a normal class for study of S. school lesson every Wednesday afternoon attended by both schools, Sunday morning prayermeeting and an hour's review of the lesson before Sunday school.

A class for the study of the Bible is held every Sabbath afternoon for nurses in the Charity Hospital. Nineteen nurses are enrolled, average attendance nine; one of the teachers assists in this work, and privately has the matron of the hospital in Bible study two evenings every week. An hour is spent in the wards of the Charity Hospital, tracts are given to patients, bedside conversations, prayermeetings in ward, and singing. Two of the patients have become Christians during the year.

The number of children who have completed the full course in the Shiba school is over fifty. Of these

    One, is a teacher in Chugakko, male.
    One, a teacher of music in Koto Jogakko, female.
    One, an artist studying in France, male.
    Two, students in Meiji Gakuin.
    Six, students in Joshi Gakuin.
    One, master builder in Hokkaido.
    One, house painter in Hokkaido.
    One, a doctor in Tokyo.
    One, engaged at Seiyoken, Ueno.
    One, engaged at Mitsui wholesale house.
    One, an official in the Tokyo Fu.
    One, a bookseller.
    One girl married a furniture dealer.
    One ,, ,, ,, teacher of the Normal School, Shidzuoka.
    One ,, ,, ,, lawyer.
    One ,, ,, ,, naval officer.

One girl a trained nurse.
One, a young man in business in Tsukiji.

The term "Christian School" is no longer a reproach but often parents bring their children asking to have them taken in because they desire to have the Christian teaching. The teachers are welcomed when they visit the homes of the children. Two deaths have occured in the Shiba school among the children. In both cases evidence of saving faith was manifested."

Miss Winn, (Osaka) writes of a primary school with 110 enrolled and 90 in average attendance under her care, saying further:—"We have added two years of the higher primary course this year in order to keep the children until the girls can enter the Naniwa Jogakko and the boys are old enough to remember more of the truth."

Kanazawa Children's School.

Statistics:
  Pupils . . 95
  Graduates . 5
  Converts . . 2

Miss Luther:—"The report for the Children's School last year was sent in during the time the local officials of this city were making their opposition to work for children felt in a practical way, refusing to grant the necessary permission to the new pupils who desired to enter the school. After several months of constant effort we won, and they have since subsided.

The difficulty cut out the entering class, so this year finds us with almost no one in the "Jinjo" second year. However, the school year was successful in many ways, and now with an increase of 18 new pupils since the opening last month, we feel another victory is won for the cause of children's work.

There seems to be among the people of this city, a growing interest in our schools. The large increase in all departments of children from good homes and the regular attendance of the same children at Sunday school, shows a more favorable attitude toward Christian schools than in the past.

At our annual commencement, when three graduated from the "Koto" department, and twelve from the "Jinjo," the Mayor was present and made a favorable address. If the lower officials leave us alone we believe we can do much for the children of this city. Two of our scholars asked for baptism during the year; one has entered a girls' school in another city and will soon be received into the church, the other is still with us and will be received somewhat later after more training entering the fold of Christ. The children continue to show an active interest in their two societies, namely, the Christian Endeavor and the Temperance League. They, under the supervision of the teachers, take charge of certain meetings, and always take part in every meeting. The daily Bible talk and Sunday school lesson, have won their way into many little hearts. One day, while out for exercise I met one of the Jinjo children, whose little brother is now in the kindergarten. She had him and a neighbor's child standing against their house, while she with Bible in hand, taught them verses she had learned in school. They were repeating Christ's words as I passed by. All seemed confused for a moment, but were reassured by my look of approval. As I went on, my heart took courage, for I saw in that act of service that His words had entered at least one child's heart.

We lost, by removal to another city last term a teacher who had been in this school ten years. Heis has been a noble service! Ever since she graduated from our Jo Gakko she has, year after year, worked constantly for this school. Her Bible lessons were a joy and blessing to all the pupils. Her help in the meetings, Sunday school, and special work has been invaluable. What a joy to find such a noble, consecrated woman, who for so many years labored for the children of her home land! Would that there were many more than there are of such workers in our schools!"

7. KINDERGARTENS.

(These are also as far as Reported Confined to the Missions of the N. Presb. Church.)

Shinagawa under Mrs. MacNair's care:—"The Shinagawa Kindergarten of forty children continues to prosper and is giving returns for the labor there expended in a steadily increasing number of the elder children and their brothers and sisters who come to the Sunday-school; and also, in the interest manifested by the mothers in the meetings and in Christian teaching. Two special evangelistic meetings were recently held in the school-room, at which audiences of from seventy to eighty quiet, attentive, adult hearers gathered as the result of the personal invitation given by the resident Bible woman in the homes of the children."

Otaru reports a kindergarten of 22 children.

Kyoto kindergartens under Miss Haworth's charge :—" The kindergartens are the " Margaret Ayres " Muromachi Maruta Machi and the " Nishijin." These have been more or less in the hands of six or more accurately two teachers. The absence of Miss Kelly and Miss Settlemeyer put them under the oversight of Dr. Alexander until Miss Haworth arrived. Four of the teachers were former students of the Joshi Gakuin. All are Christians.

The March commencement graduated 35 pupils from the two schools which together have an actual attendance of 80 as reported to the government. Many applicants have been refused admission after taking as many as had left on certificates. Both schools are in a good condition in some but not in all respects. They are important adjuncts to the church and our work giving a strong hold on a non-Christian community.

A daily prayer-meeting has been formed for the teachers and it is hoped from this will grow daily meetings for mothers who chanced to come in.

The teachers of each school meet at the close of the work for Bible reading and prayer, at their respective places. Urgent need of a higher primary department is shown in the number of graduates that go out and a comparatively large number of applicants too old for the kindergarten who are refused. Special pains have been taken of late to meet the parents, particularly the mothers. Many homes have been visited and the gospel way prepared. Very interesting experiences have shown in this relation how soon reward may come with prayer, effort and devotion, the omission of any one of which has marred the harmony and defeated the end in this as well as greater works if greater there be.

The Margant Ayres kindergarten is made happy by foreign visitors every now and then and a pleasing attitude on the part of patrons.

The Nishijin lies out of the way of the tourist which prevents advantages due it as well.

The commencements at the two places were attractive and an appreciative audience both foreign and Japanese were present.

The running expenses of the Kindergartens are met by the receipts while the mission pays rents and salaries."

STATISTICS:

Pupils	90
Foreign teachers	1
Japanese	7

Yamaguchi.

STATISTICS:

Pupils	23
Foreign teachers	1
Japanese ,,	3

MRS. AYRES:—Since September the kindergarten here, has been under my supervision and has had a fairly prosperous year; there are 23 children in actual attendance, and two teachers with one assistant, lately taken on. We have held monthly mothers' meetings, which have only been moderately well attended.

Kanazawa:—Miss Luther:—"Our cry for the kindergarten is, "More room," "More helpers." We have turned away more than twenty applicants since April 1st. We had a graduating class of twelve in March. Their places and all other vacant places are filled, still we have had to turn away many wishing to enter. The commencement exercises were full of interest to parents, who composed the larger part of the audience, and children who took their various parts with vim. Rainbow wearing by the girls in the graduating class and a soldier-boy march and song, with guns, horses and flags, by the boys, seemed the leading items on the program, although the march and games held the interest of all. Not as many of these children, who represent homes of the military officials stationed here, attend the Sunday school as we would like to see, yet we feel that there is here also a deeper interest than a year ago. One father is now a regular attendant at church services. The head teacher is very faithful in visiting among the mothers; so it is a common thing to see mothers at the school visiting her after school hours are over. We consider this a very encouraging line of work, and are surprised that more young women are not desirous of entering kindergarten work. No interference on the part of officials makes it easier to carry on the work, and the influence gained over these little lives during the three years they are in the kindergarten is very great. Who can tell the result of such influence in after years!"

G. INDUSTRIAL EDUCATION.

MRS. MACNAIR:—"A sewing-school was started this spring as a private venture by Mrs. MacNair in the hope of gaining a more permanent interest with the young women of Shinagawa. At the time of writing six pupils are in attendance. A graduate of the most celebrated sewing-school in Tokyo and a former resident in the Training School for Bible-women is in charge, and we have every reason to hope for a good school in the Autumn."

MISS CASE writes about her cooking class in which she has been greatly interested:—

"An increasing interest has also been felt among the 30 members of the cooking class which is composed of the wives of judges, doctors and others occupying prominent positions."

A part of her work is in industrial classes in needlework, flower arrangement, etiquette &c., carried on in the Sumiyoshicho school building under the auspices of Shiloh Church.

MRS. AYRES:—"A woman's meeting and cooking class in which Miss Palmer and I work together, has been kept up with semi-monthly meetings."

MR. BRYAN:—"The work in Matsuyama has been mostly among the women and a cooking class has been largely the means of reaching a good number of wives. Eight ladies from the cooking class are studying the Bible preparatory to baptism."

Mrs. Winn has three cooking classes for women. She also frequently treats persons with electricity: this often affords opportunity to influence such persons for Christ. She further writes:—"The women have lately shown as much interest in foreign cooking as the young men have in English and so I have tried by this means to reach many women whom I could in no other way gain any influence over. I am most thankful, for the women who have thus heard become truly interested so that they come to Sabbath services bringing friends with them and often influencing their husbands to hear also.

Two most encouraging cases of this sort have recently occurred at Sakai. The husband of one died a few weeks ago giving good evidence of being a true Christian just before his death, and requesting a Christian funeral."

Mrs. Peeke has classes in knitting and English with accompanying Bible study twice a week, reaching also teachers and pupils of the Normal school thereby. She further instructs some of the Christian women in the Old Testament.

Mrs. Scudder has a knitting class of 50 girls who manifest much interest and receive regular religious instruction.

MRS. JONES:—" A cooking class was tried but did not prove a sufficient attraction." No doubt it will take some time before Fukui can appeal to a foreignized palate such as Yokohama does now.

A good deal more of this kind of work is done. The above must be taken as samples only.

II. NIGHT CLASSES.

Of these evidently only a few specimens are reported. Three night classes for young men are held Mrs. Winn.

Miss Winn and Miss Wycoff report an interesting case as follows:— "Last winter two of our Christian young men were troubled by the lack of interest in their Y. M. C. A. and decided to open a night school hoping thus to get hold of more young men. They promised that if we would teach English, *they* would be responsible for teaching translation and the Japanese branches. What was at first an experiment has proved a success. This night school does not cost the mission a cent of money and is proving a very important feature of our work. There are now more than 40 names enrolled. Many attend the services and 4 have asked for baptism, and have joined the preparatory class."

Dr. Hail of Wakayama reports a night school and an orphanage in which the pastor and missionary are asked to lecture on morals and religion.

Mr. McILWAINE:—"In order to get those young men who are specially anxious to learn English under Christian influence a night school for English has been started under the auspices of the church or rather pastor. Both he and his assistant teach in it besides another teacher (non-Christian) from the Chu Gakko, the missionary also assisting. A tuition fee of 50 *sen* per month and a matriculation fee of 1 *yen* are charged. This institution was begun on May 1st and so we cannot give results yet."

I. ENGLISH CLASSES.

These run along the same line as the night classes as far as the missionary is concerned. Only samples are reported. Let us preface this by a remark from Mr. Peeke:—"We feel down here that the day when it is necessary to use baits is drawing to a close. In fact we are persuaded that no missionary is warranted in teaching English till the language has been mastered. We are confident that if missionaries will only desist from English teaching till the language is mastered, they will then have so many opportunites for simple and direct religious work that they will not think for a moment of wasting valuable strength in indirect methods. It takes courage to apply this principle, but it is well to insist on it. Don't do it ourselves yet, *i.e.* wife does not; but we are coming on."

Mr. SCUDDER reports teaching a class of policemen in English, most of whom come also to an English Bible class on Sundays and then remain through the preaching service. Several have become earnest inquirers. Through this Bible class too he has won many young men to attend church, a good number having become Christians. Mrs. Scudder took a similar Bible class in a neighboring town thus opening a new place to Christian work, where 2 persons have become Christians and about a dozen, inquirers. The text book is the Bible rather than the 2nd Reader, and thus applications for English are easily dealt with. Besides this Mr. Scudder has obtained good results through singing classes, using not only the church hymns but also anthems and other music more pretentious than hymns. Not only has this helped church services, but even a sacred concert has been held. After every morning service, a half hour of social song is greatly enjoyed by many. Certainly missionaries of musical ability might thus learn to appreciate one of their special gifts by applying it more fully to service to the gratification and upbuilding of many.

Mrs. Scudder reports one English Bible class of men, all school teachers, and one for Normal school girls.

Perhaps one of the most successful pieces of work in English teaching is done by Miss Case among the young business men of Yokohama. 7-9 o'clock in the morning before the office hours of the day open is the time chosen. Thus with minds fresh and earnest, and accompanied by spirited singing, good results in English are attained. Moreover the religious element in the daily routine is emphasized, especially so in an English Bible class on Sundays of an average attendance of 24 and in a special monthly evening meeting.

Miss Gardner, Miss Milliken, Dr. Wyckoff, Mr. Landis and many others probably do work in English Bible class teaching outside of their school work in this line.

Mrs. Myers reports an English class imposing the condition that all who enter also attend church services, a condition so well kept so far that when she fails to meet her class one week, the girls interpret their part of the contract literally and in good part stay away from the succeeding service. Old pupils bring in recruits and so the attendance at church profits too. Some seed will likely fall on good ground.

Miss Ella Gardner took on request in English a class of young men using the Bible. She says, " I was surprised to find them able to converse intelligently and to ask thoughtful questions. I hope to lead its members to the Saviour. The girls' class in my house has numbered from 25 to 50 all the year."

J. SUNDAY SCHOOLS.

Here we are encroaching on the more technically known evangelistic work.

First to be noted is the great need of emphasis upon this department of mission and church work. Perhaps we have not fully appreciated our opportunity here. Statistics seem to show that some churches, the Methodist for example, are far ahead of us in appreciating this nursery of the church. Still this year's statistics reveal a marked improvement along this line, there being 8415 S. S. members a gain of 2207 over 6208 as reported last year, or 35% increase.

"The Sunday School offers greater chances than ever before as real training schools for the children and if there is any one point more than another that deserves the special attention of the Council it is the question of providing more literature of a high class for the children, and to assist those who are engaged in work with young people. In our zeal to reform we have not laid enough stress upon the importance of work for the individual in the formative period of life.

We would do well to take heed to these words of an earnest Sunday School worker at home,—

'The wise missionary, like the wise worker at home, cannot afford to treat with even partial indifference the boundless opportunity and the supreme claims of child-life. The future glorious church of the Sunrise Kingdom must be made up largely of those who are children to-day.'

Shall we not give more thought to this part of the work in the future than has been given to it in the past?"

DR. A. D. HAIL:—"The Sunday Schools also indicate growth. In each of our churches it is necessary to have two Sunday schools in order to accommodate the attendance. In the morning the church-members, young men and women, and the children of the church meet for Bible study. In the afternoon the children of the neighborhoods are gathered in. These latter schools are well attended. They furnish a field of work for the scholars in our girls' school who have shown not only a commendable zeal in taking up such work, but also real capability in conducting and developing these schools under their respective superintendents."

In the second place, let us not forget the fact that our S. schools are furnished with a series of helps equal to the best published anywhere perhaps. This involves a financial deficit every year but this is as nothing if the blessing is properly appreciated and utilized. One member of the Council along with those of other Missions devotes a good deal of time to the preparation of these helps. These helps have outside of the Episcopal Church a practical monopoly of the field, and they are published at a rate such that every church S. school at least ought to be able to afford the price. The missionary can do much in many ways, especially in thoroughly preparing himself and gathering the teachers and others for a Normal class, also by his presence and active participation, if possible, in the S. schools themselves, and by influencing the pastors to see their privileges along these lines. Every missionary ought to make a point of studying these helps in Japanese. He would get a double benefit in doing so. Does every one of our Council get a copy of the Teachers' Monthly? If not let him or her send 40 sen at once to the Methodist Publishing House.

Still another idea is given by Mr. Peeke, who writes, "Our Christians in this field are pretty well scattered. In order to bind them together I have started an adaptation of the Home Department of the S. school idea. I manage it by mail, using the union Quarterlies. The contribution and report envelopes of the 1st quarter have come in quite satisfactorily, though it will take a year to find out whether the thing will really work. The idea is a good one, I feel sure, and could be worked with profit in other places."

Mr. Scudder has this suggestion, "I used to buy colored picture cards using then to make little friends and to attract children to our various S. schools. Last year instead of buying them I made a request through our church paper that S. schools would send me what were left over from their supply. The result has been that I have received an abundant supply free of cost and have also quite unexpectedly enlisted the interest of several S. schools and societies in America in our work, and increased their general interest in missions."

Many of our missionaries especially among the ladies, directly and indirectly, are deeply interested in S. school work, some teaching, others superintending, some gathering poor children off the streets, and in various ways trying to sow the seed.

Mrs. Scudder reports 9 S. schools with an attendance of 500 pupils in winter and 400 in spring under her general care assisted by a helper and two other Christians. Miss Winn reports five, Mrs. Winn 3; Mrs. Hope, one, and though only 2 children belong to the church she has gathered into the church a flourishing S. school; Mrs. Ayres, 1; Mrs. Myers reports a union Christmas entertainment of S. schools of all denomination in Tokushima, proving a great success in many ways.

Mr. Buchanan writes:—"The Sunday schools in Takamatsu are in a rather encouraging condition. The main one is well attended and the missionaries all teach regularly in this, as we have not enough teachers in our young Christians to do this work. A good number of the adult Christians attend the Bible class taught by one of the missionaries. One of the delightful features of our work is the spirit of hopeful humility that characterizes this little body of Christians. Early last spring they earnestly requested to be taught on Sabbath afternoons as well as in the morning Bible class. So another class was formed and the study of Romans was taken up, this class also being taught by a missionary.

The other Sunday school in the city amounts to a children's meeting and is efficiently conducted by the evangelist and his family in the chapel, in which they reside."

Miss Ella Gardner writes about a S. school teachers' meeting held at her house once a week. Mr. and Mrs. Lampe and Mr. Faust write of their efforts in S. school lines.

S. schools for poor or street children are superintended by many. Mrs. Wyckoff has one such meeting in her own house, Mrs. Landis has one whose members up to 70 often crowd the little room to the utmost. Unfortunately recently a teacher in the public school seems to use his influence in preventing children from coming.

Again there are many S. schools assisted through those in charge of boarding schools directing and instructing their pupils in such work. The Joshi Gakuin for example assists quite a number of S. schools. Bible women too find here one of their choice spheres of interest and usefulness.

Mr. McIlwaine of Kochi calls attention to an unfortunate phase. While the S. school there has good attendance, it is regarded as for children only and worse still as all-sufficient for them being made a substitute for attendance upon church services. It is sad to see some 50-60 boys and girls from 10-16 trooping out of church to play on the street or seek other amusement when the morning service begins and their parents assemble for worship. Such a practice if general calls for attention from the leaders. It is to be feared that Kochi children are not altogether exceptional in this respect.

EVANGELISTIC WORK.

In this department, we shall begin with the South-west and shall proceed most readily by missions,—in other words travel from Peeke to Pierson.

SOUTH JAPAN MISSION OF THE R. C. A.

Kiushiu, STATIONS:—Nagasaki, Saga, Kumamoto, Kagoshima.

MR. PEEKE, KAGOSHIMA:—"We have a compact field, cut off by mountains and rather difficult of access; a peculiar dialect that makes it difficult to work for the rural classes; no hindrances worth mentioning except the one common to all Japan, lack of helpers, and also lack of funds to employ them, work hopeful, several young men baptized. We worked in 1901 with other denomination in Taikyo Dendo, but will now strengther our special lines. Location of church in Kagoshima is A 1, new comers at every service and passers by come in to listen. S. school well organized, using the union lesson helps with good results. Mrs. Peeke teaches an English Bible class in it; 2 other S. schools besides that of the church. Preaching in an open *kogisho*. This and Taikyo Dendo is more of the nature of seed sowing than of reaping. Together with the C. M. S. and M. E. people, we have held 50 Taikyo Dendo meetings."

MR. PIETERS, KUMAMOTO:—"The work here is under the Home Mission Board and seems proceeding a little better than the average; a fine nucleus for a church; having almost no students it is more stable than a congregation of students but there is not enough aggressive evangelism in it. Taikyo Dendo resulted in over 400 asking for instruction; these were distributed among pastors, but of earnest inquirers hardly any are left,—a great disappointment. The same is the case with the Mott meetings; magnificently successful in assembling young men, many declaring themselves ready to follow Christ, but visible results 4 mos. later were almost nothing. Still all these meetings did good in scattering seed, and no doubt some fruit will yet ripen. The Y. M. C. A. in the Koto Gakko here is said to be divided because of the "New Theology" under the influence of Mr. Ebina on Christ's Divinity. Danger from heresy is very real especially where our members come in contact with Kumiai members."

Mr. Oltomans, Saga :—" Much seed sowing has been done, several new preaching places opened, a number of baptisms, and the general attitude of outsiders is that of inquiry. Taikyo Dendo received much attention but results as far as visible are not very reassuring. Taikyo Dendo has had good effects on Christians. But all results therefrom will largely depend on more Taikyo Dendo to follow. As far as we can see, we need the *Tokyo* style of Taikyo Dendo. I have had 2 Bible classes among Chu Gakko and Normal school students."

Mission of the Southern Presbyterian Church.

Shikoku, Stations:—Kochi, Susaki, Takamatsu, and Tokushima.

Main island, Stations:—Kobe, Gifu, Nagoya, Okazaki, Toyohashi, Tokyo.

Mr. McIlwaine, Kochi:—" Encouraging year on the whole. Taikyo Dendo did not reach here, but we had Shokyo Dendo which promises good results. Kochi church employs an assistant pastor, a step forward enabling it to do more evangelistic work. Some special services were held and people are anxious to hear the gospel. The pastor and assistant have work also at three country places. The pastor has a weekly class for inquirers and several have received baptism. The Y. M. C. A. of the church feels the stimulus of Secretary Fisher's visit and Mr. Uno's meetings which led Chugakko students to a study of Christianity. A few have come to the missionary on difficult points. Miss Atkinson kept up two children's meetings and visited much, but is now in the Kanazawa Girls School. Mrs. McIlwaine has a children's meeting in an Eta village. She visits, distributes tracts, sells gospels, &c.

Motoyama pays half the preachers' salary and some Christians are so active as to go with the evangelist to neighboring villages assisting in various ways.

Aki was selfsupporting (though not a church) till last spring, but had a setback due largely to fraud of one member who now is in prison, and this place now seeks help from the Mission.

The missionary visits other groups of Christians.

Frequent evidence of work done here and elsewhere, even as far back as 15-20 years ago, meets one and such persons show interest and knowledge when spoken to ; such need the quickening of the Holy Spirit so as to obey the truth. To get people to say they will study Christianity is not hard but obedience is exceedingly difficult. Many study but few enter the church. Still a number have been baptized at every bimonthly communion service; some of these have come from the country, the pastor preferring to baptize in the church.

I kept up the practice of carrying gospels and New Testaments on evangelistic trips selling over 300 copies. Miss Atkinson also sold. Mr. Lawrence of the Bible society sold about 3000 on a visit in February. Two colporters also sold many. A higher standard of life or rather a closer conformity to the one they have is imperatively needed."

Mr. Moore of Susaki returned on furlough in spring and no report has been received.

MISS DOWD, KOCHI and KOBE:—"Miss Dowd's principal work has been Bible classes, city and country evangelistic work. The Bible classes are taught in Kochi from January until July. The women from the country as well as city attend these. The chief object of these classes has been to encourage and to prepare the Christian women to do personal work and to teach Sabbath school classes. Personal work has been the leading study. On Sunday she has had a large class of elderly women known as "obasan" (elderly women). A student of the Bible classes held several years ago organized this class and taught it. While Miss Dowd was in Kobe she began with Genesis and they finished Leviticus a few weeks ago. There are usually 28 present at this Bible class. These women, for they are not all "obasan" visit and do a good deal of work. To reach the student class, her Bible women have had 22 organ pupils. These have been taught the Bible daily. The English class was not so well attended. Miss Dowd gives the Fall months to long country trips. In her visiting she has met girls that she felt must be helped to support themselves. She has had an industrial work on a small scale for five of these girls. They have had daily Bible classes, reading and singing. They have worked most of the day on knitting and sewing machines and other sewing. Miss Dowd has been delighted with the progress of the girls. They know that they can study only so much as they can earn the money themselves for."

MR. MYERS, TOKUSHIMA:—"As secretary of the Mission, I will first mention a few general items of the S. Presb. work.

Rev. S. R Hope returned from furlough, and was stationed in Toyohashi, Mikawa province.

Miss Sala Evans and Miss Charlotte Sterling returned recently The latter has been in America several years. She has been stationed in Nagoya to teach in the Kinjo Jogakko.

Rev. J. Wallace Moore and family have gone home on furlough.

Miss L. E. Wimbish was moved to Kobe for her health, but has since had to go home.

Rev. C. K. Cumming has been moved from Nagoya to Gifu, and Gifu has been constituted a separate station.

Foreign houses have been built for Rev. Wm. C. Buchanan in Takamatsu and the Misses Patton in Tokushima. Our Mission's policy now is to provide comfortable foreign homes for each missionary as far as possible.

At our last annual Mission meeting a committee appointed to prepare a "catechism for candidates" reported recommending that prepared by Rev. D. Thompson, D.D. This catechism "is distinctly Presbyterian, and covers very well the grounds that our Mission would desire specially to be taught."

Owing to the indefiniteness in the word "outstation," it was defined as "a place where Christians reside and work is done, or where services are held at least six times a year."

Our mission entered into coöperation with the Theological Department of the Meiji Gakuin, and Rev. S. P. Fulton was chosen our representative in this institution.

Members of our mission have at last been constituted a legal person and can now hold property in Japan. The application was made finally on the lines adopted by the East Japan Presbyterian Mission.

We united with the C. M. S. workers in Taikyo Dendo in July and in October. There was good attendance and quite a number of inquirers, of whom a few retain their interest and a number are ready to listen when visited. In this and all our relations with the C. M. S. we can thank God for unity rather than bewail the lack of it.

We have here two small lady missionaries and one married couple, two Bible women and 3 evangelists, (1 in the city, 1, 7 miles south and 1, 45 miles west). We have regular services in 8 other places and occasional services in many others.

In the city we supplement the *kogisha* (preaching place) system by renting a room in an unworked quarter, holding nightly services for some days. As one good result, I notice that I am called Myers San instead of *Ketojin* as elsewhere."

Miss Patton, Tokushima, reports good attendance at meetings for women and children, a number of women being interested.

W. C. BUCHANAN, TAKAMATSU (on behalf of the workers in Sanuki):—" Work lost numerically ; only 10 adults received into church since May 1901, while 21 from Takamatsu and 15 from Zentsuji have moved away, 20 going to Tokyo (16 to the same section of Tokyo forming quite a colony). All these were wide awake Christians and we hear good reports for the most part. Our pastor has gone to Chiba as pastor, a great loss to us, and so most of the preaching in the city has fallen to the foreigners. Attendance at services is good and no falling off in spite of removals. With 40 Christians we have from 55 to 73 attendants at services.

We always have street preaching. We have also recently held a series of special meetings for the crowds who attended the Industrial Exhibition from April 11—May 30. In a good sized arbor we had daily preaching from 2-5 or 6 P.M. Others in and outside of the Mission, Japanese and foreigners, gave valuable assistance.

The ladies conduct 2 classes, one for teachers of the Higher Girls School, and the other for school girls. The weekly woman's meeting shows great interest in raising funds for the church building, about 10 raising 40 yen outside of the regular contributions. In order to cultivate a spirit of helpfulness among the Christian women we employ no Bible woman, and the plan succeeds admirably. In an outstation with few Christians, a Bible woman does excellent work. Both lady missionaries teach in S. school and visit.

Zentsuji is the most important place outside of Takamatsu ; all our Christians were connected with the garrison and the prison work and so when the government dispensed with military prisons there, these Christians with others were dismissed and moved elsewhere, and unfortunately the Christians remaining are of the inferior kind. The evangelist there is faithful. He was taken from Nagao where the one Christian couple still keep up the Sunday school. Preaching services are held here and in many towns throughout the province. Our great need is more workers."

MR. PRICE, KOBE:—" No special features, but favorable progress alon, the usual [...] in an open port. Seventy adults added, about half by letter, and half by confession, the largest number on record. Prospects for growth in Hiogo are good, and we hope to have a church in a few year[s]. Hiogo has 80000 people and only one church. Mr. Hattori, an experienced and earnest minister, works there. Last October we began work in the east end of 48000 people with no church or worker. This resulted in the best chapel I ever had in Japan, but the lack of a Japanese worker prevents the reaping in full there. This lack is a chief obstacle. From recent experience I would urge the use of cards signed by those who desire to be taught (a feature of Tokyo Dendo). Thus one can follow up by visits, tracts or letters. Liberal use of the mail will go far to supply lack of visits. The missionary can do more visiting than has been the custom, and with good results. A Bible class for the grammer school teachers is held at their request, in English first, followed by a Japanese lesson.

The work of the ladies has been along the usual lines and the regret is their inability to fully size upon all opportunities.

The three things most needed seem to be,—

1. More workers.
2. More consecration and devotion on the part of church members.
3. A better realization of the duty resting on our church for the evangelization of Japan and a closer drawing together in Christian unity.

The close relation between mission work and Christian work for foreigners does not seem to be realized. If we could get strong active Protestant churches for foreigners in the ports, the mission work in the ports and the country at large would feel it greatly. Such churches would also be a great blessing to the foreigners and their home lands. There should be some way to interest the foreign communities in direct mission work. Moreover the wrong impressions of tourists could be thus prevented. A booklet on mission and church work for distribution among tourists, might be prepared by committees in the open ports and Tokyo and distributed.

After nearly two years, of tedious and prolonged effort the men connected with the Southern Presbyterian Church, were formed into a juridical person to own land and houses to aid in propagating Christianity, one official showing special helpfulness in this work.

Great delay in Kobe in obtaing permission to open new chapels is very inconvenient and difficult to understand. An application in October has not been granted yet (June). Still there has been preaching all this time. Some of us would greatly desire more stations opened by the Cooperating Missions."

MR. CUMMING, GIFU:—"During the year we have moved from Nagoya to Gifu. My country work is the same as when in Nagoya, but Gifu being a better center for this, we moved hither. Besides the Gifu work seemed to need the presence of a foreigner.

In Gifu the work is improving. The Christians are not many, church services were poorly attended and the prayer meeting had died. The prayermeeting has been resuscitated and church attendance is improving greatly. I have a *Shitsumonkwai* on Mondays, not very well attended. Mrs. Cumming has a class of students on Sundays and a weekly class of young ladies in English including Bible instruction.

Recently she was asked to take a class of the teachers of the Girls School of Gifu, but the conservative anti-Christian feeling of the people was too strong. Some official heard the girls singing a Christian time. Reporting the matter, the principal of the school was called before the city authorities, and the girls were told to sing no Christian hymns or tunes. Now however the school has come under the control of the prefecture and so it may soon have greater liberties.

My country work has two centers besides 3 points connected with the Gifu work, and two additional country centers where evangelists live, making 14 or 15 places in the Gifu field. At Ogaki I lately formed an English Bible class for the Chugakko teachers, eight attending.

Recently Hon. K. Kataoka and Mr. Kiyama visited one of my country fields expressly to make Christian addresses. Many of the better class came to hear and we hope for much good.

There is a great lack in Sabbath keeping, and this point is urged upon them though without much appreciation as yet of its importance."

MR. MCALPINE, NAGOYA:—" Probably Taikyo Dendo has been the most prominent matter of the year, yet as up to this time not a single Christian from this work has been added to our churches in Nagoya, the result seems disappointing. Still there are results neither few nor small.

1 Union of all Christian churches in prayer, planning and active

daily preaching as never before. They have passed the stage of mere formal resolutions to pray for union, and have practical union in actual fact. True, it is not called federated union nor is any one formally bound to continue it. It is union arising from the heart, the only real union.

2 It has given the Christians courage and confidence in the final success of the cause. The year's successes have infused courage to hope for much and to work in earnest according to such faith.

3 It has enlightened the general public about Christianity not a little, many thousands have heard for the first time, many have become serious enough to hand in this names. Only a small percentage has as yet been baptized. The remainder can hardly be regarded as backsliders, rather as sympathizers, favorably disposed to the gospel, and many in an earnest hour may yet turn to the gospel for light and salvation.

In my special work there is much to encourage,—baptisms, and inquirers some of whom are applicants for baptism. The Christians are more earnest and awake than for several years. Some backsliders are returning. A church building fund has been started and is growing.

A dissension in the church here brought its spiritual life to a low ebb, but the breach has been healed, and the condition is fair again. Seto church is getting new life, and a leading member, a doctor has built up a real live S. school.

We plan to work along the new railway to Nakatsugawa. There is a good deal of street preaching.

1902 seems likely to prove a better year than last. On 2 country trips, one with Mr. Fulton,—we had good audiences, showing the people more ready to hear than ever before."

MR. HOPE, TOYOHASHI:—"A new station, the largest city in Mikawa province. We began work here Jan. 25,1902. No strong prejudices, the chief obstacle so common now being an inordinate desire for wealth. A Bible class in my home on Sunday morning goes also to the service in the church. I have also a Bible class of army officers reading in English but explaining in Japanese. However most of these will not go to church services. One was baptized recently who formerly hated the Christian religion.

In Okazaki a good number were recently added to the church, doubtless the fruit of Mr. Fulton's long and faithful work there.

Mrs. Hope organized a Sunday school and conducts a woman's prayer-meeting. The women are interested in raising money for a church building, doing fancy work and contributing liberally of their money."

MR. FULTON, OKAZAKI and TOKYO:—"Mr. Fulton' work is now partly educational and partly evangelistic. After careful consultation with the Missions controlling the Meiji Gakuin, the S. Presb. Mission joined in the Theo. Dept. Elected as the representative of this Mission, Mr. Fulton moved thither to take up the work. New Testament work falls to his lot, New Testament introduction and the interpretation of Acts and I Cor.; also a class in English for the preparatory year.

Besides teaching he has a good deal of preaching in Tokyo and vicinity, giving also assistance in Taikyo Dendo services. He thinks that the interest in Tokyo is not so general as last year, and that this movement will have to be guarded against some unhealthy features. In all such work there is danger of its degenerating into mere noise with no permanent results.

Besides the above he makes monthly visits to Okazaki, his former field and serves also on the "Standing Committee of Cooperating Missions."

Mrs. Fulton assists in a Sunday school, and visits in the congregation.

In Okazaki there is still a strong drift against Christianity. A special effort was made to reach the young men, by organizing Bible classes. The schools of Okazaki are indifferent or hostile. Christian teachers in both Normal and High school will not come to church or identify themselves with us. Recently opposition stopped several teachers from coming to study Christianity.

Taikyo Dendo meetings have been productive of much good in Okazaki. The semi-annual evangelists' meeting made special efforts in theater *enzetsu* (lecture meetings), and with advertisements, invitations to prominent people, walking the streets with flag and bell, &c, gave us an audience of 500 with splendid attention. These meetings resulted in the giving in of many names, helping some to decide, bringing out the Christians and making them see their duty to non-Christian neighbors.

The women have raised 500 *yen* toward a church. This is to be built this year yet and together with funds otherwise raised will cost about 1000 yen. Several Bible classes were conducted. Since last Fall 20 persons have been baptized in Okazaki.

Besides Toyohashi where Mr. Hope is now, the only other place with a band of Christians is Tsugu.

Miss Wimbiseh after being laid aside by sickness for more than a year was obliged to return to America without prospect of returning."

CUMBERLAND PRESBYTERIAN MISSION.

STATIONS:—Osaka, Wakayama, Ise, Shingu, Takatsuki, Tanabe.

DR. A. D. HAIL, OSAKA:—" I have found much willingness among increased numbers to hear and to inquire about the gospel. The Christians have felt the inspirations of the 20th century movement, and in Yokkaichi, Ise, Matsuzaka and Yamada, Christians have shown growing interest in work. Workers from Nagoya, Osaka and Tokyo have inspired them. As results we have an increased number of baptisms, and more earnest efforts by the Christians to reach their neighbors.

In Osaka churches, methods have been almost revolutionized, and the spiritual life deepened. While all have shared in this blessing, young men especially feel their obligations to Christ and His Church; young men are in the majority among those gathered in. Thus the young men are organizing better for aggressive efforts.

In Yamada where are the great Ise shrines, it takes great courage to cast in one's lot with his fellow Christians. Some moving thither from other churches, fail to take part in worship and in efforts to bring others to Christ. Some thus go lost.

In some places it is difficult to get a regular *kyōgisho* (preaching place).

The work as a whole furnishes ground for special encouragement and thanksgiving."

MR. VAN HORNE, OSAKA:—" My work embraces 2 chapels in Osaka and 12 towns in the provinces, Settsu, Izumi, and Kii. In Osaka and almost all other points the work is more prosperous than ever before, services and S. school are well attended, and attendance is increasing. Still the immediate results are not as great as desired, though far in advance of previous years. We are entering good homes near our chapels, and in consequence have some women inquirers. Formerly our congregations were mostly men. I have English classes to teach the Bible, and many soon show a great interest in the Bible.

Outside Osaka work varies, in some, deep and growing interest, in others where most efforts are made, the people remain untouched. Still we try to break through the wall of superstition and heathenism. We have a greater number to study the Bible than ever before, have baptized a good number, and slowly gather some fruits of Taikyo Dendo. The results from Taikyo Dendo do not fill out one's wishes. This year's effort in Osaka was very quiet, only 2 evening meetings at each church, well advertised, well attended as a rule, and preaching evangelical. There seems a lack of dependence on Divine assistance, faith in prayer is very indefinite, too much stress is laid on *gakumon* and long sermons, many of our former evangelists have become worldly and do not attend church. Of those educated by our own mission, I know of five, once effective workers who now seldom or never attend services. These all would be re-employed if they desired it and showed themselves sincere. Also many of the laity once regular and devoted, are never seen now at church. And this state of things is all too general, a very discouraging feature and especially as this dead material often comes between us and the people."

MRS. VAN HORNE:—" My work is the same but methods are varied to meet the conditions, fewer meetings and more visiting so as to reach the women and get them out to meetings. To believe they must hear, to hear, a teacher is needed, and we have to become teachers going to them or else they will not have any. This work brings rich reward, and more women are interested now than ever before."

MISS ALEXANDER, TAKATSUKI:—"I am engaged in evangelistic work in the country, and after a year's absence am impressed with the desire of Christians for a deeper spiritual life, and their feeling of a duty to the unconverted. People generally show a more genuine interest than formerly. The spirit of investigation is gaining, and prejudices are weakening. While there have always been more open doors than we could enter, yet to-day is in a special sense the day of opportunity."

MISS ELLA GARDNER, TANABE:—" Work here is well organized and harmonious. The Bible class is well attended, some being careful students of the Bible and attending services. Our pastor who is in charge of a general reading room for young men, is allowed to put in Christian reading and we have put in Christian books and papers which are eagerly read. With attending services, Sunday School and prayermeeting, teaching an English Bible class of young men and a girls' class of from 30 to 50, giving out tracts and loaning books, calling and receiving calls, the weeks are pretty full.

Dr. J. B. Hail, Wakayama:—"The work here is intimately connected with that of the church of Christ. Four organized churches in the ken; two, Wakayama and Tanabe having pastors, but not able to pay their whole salary, the Mission employs half their time, one thus visiting regularly 8, and the other, 10 towns; another, Shingu, has a licentiate, paying ⅔ of his salary and the Mission employing ⅓ of his time spent in visiting 5 towns. Airin has no pastor being served from Wakayama.

Wakayama and Tanabe churches show a net gain of one each, Shingu gaining 5, and Airin 12. Still there were 29 baptisms in all 4 churches, whose combined membership is 288, or 222 adults; they own property worth 2,730 *yen* and contributed 846 *yen* for all purposes. Tanabe church is best organized and Airin is most aggressive. Mr. Worley moved to Shingu, reorganized the Sunday school while the ladies began children's meetings in the towns and adjacent villages. A Y. M. C. A. of 40 members was organized by Mr. Worley and Dr. Oishi. Tanabe has two evangelistic bands consisting of the men and the women respectively, the men going out by twos and the women in larger companies. Airin, in Hikata has a like band, meeting for prayer at 2 again after the Sunday morning service; then they go out by twos into districts apportioned, visiting every house and inviting all to church. Distributing 50 copies of the "Toki no Koe" in one district, they collect them again in two weeks to redistribute them in the second leaving new ones in the first district, and so on until the copies are worn out after visiting 7 or 8 families. Thus the visitors receive a cordial welcome, and one result is that the little church building's capacity is too small, while there are 4 meetings also in different parts of the town for Bible study and prayer. In Wakayama a class for reaching the young was organized, English being taught, lectures given on religion and other themes and recreation provided. So far there are 30 members, fees, &c., being 85 *sen* per month. Many of these come to Sunday school and church.

Outside work is encouraging in every way, two villages through their headmen even asking for visits and for preaching of the gospel, one at the instance of a business man and the other at that of a Buddhist priest, and resulting in large audiences,—600 where the Buddhist priest favored us, who also urged the people to investigate the claims of the gospel.

All the pastors report a number of inquirers. House-to-house work is kept up. Mrs. Hail keeps up the woman's meeting, once a month being an all day meeting for work whose proceeds go to the church. She has also a Sunday school and a children's meeting on Saturday; these work and send proceeds to the Okayama orphanage."

MR. JOHN F. HAIL, ISE:—"My work during the first part of last year was in the Osaka field. Here there has been a number of converts, mostly young men of a quite solid type.

At Nagano several Christians have been baptized. Here a little band of Christians, now seven in number, holds services every Saturday and Sunday in a Buddhist temple. Hirano, a peculiarly hard place, has seen three baptisms.

The last part of this past year I have been in Tsu, Ise, working through part of the Ise field. Besides several baptisms, one is struck with the number of solid thinking men here who are inquirers. This is especially remarkable when one remembers the past record of this section in its bitter opposition to Christianity. Undoubtedly He who holds the hearts of the people in His hands, is moving the hearts of this people toward Himself."

MR. WORLEY, SHINGU:—"Sickness disturbed our work but we have tried our best. Though in the interior there is a good church here. I have helped in Sunday school and did special work among young men with some good results, made a tour last spring with an evangelist, having meetings each night and distributing scripture portions and tracts. The pastor goes monthly on such tours. Had eight accessions, but due to changes of residence the church remains the same about. This my second year in Japan went largely into language study. Mrs. Worley works among women and had well attended Bible classes weekly."

WEST JAPAN MISSION OF THE PRESBYTERIAN CHURCH (NORTH.)

STATIONS:—Matsuyama, Yamaguchi, Hiroshima, Osaka, Kyoto, Kanazawa, and Fukui.

MR. BRYAN, MATSUYAMA:—"Sickness of the evangelist has largely interferred with Taikyo Dendo plans but quiet work with individuals yielded gratifying results. A layman for Ozu has gotten out to church many nonattending members, and audiences increased fourfold. A politician invited us to his village and 18 persons joined the Scripture Union earnestly studying the Bible. Through this man, influential and earnest for himself and friends, work is to open in a neighboring village. He brought 2 nurses who come here for Bible study while studying in Matsuyama. Mrs. Bryan and I made talks to nurses at the provincial hospital and we hope to get entrance into this hospital. One opportunity utilized brings others, and so days are busy and the number we meet increases.

(This is about the best I can do. I hate reports and as I said at mission meeting, 'after hearing the reports of 7 inch guns and rapid firing machines it will be a rest to hear the report of a popgun.')"

MR. AYRES, YAMAGUCHI:—"No changes in the personnel of the working force, except that the Yamaguchi pastor has gone to Kobe, and I supply his place. They are looking for a pastor but can hardly raise enough money. This church has for some years been independent of mission aid. We need a good Bible woman or two even more than a man. This is pretty strong but we want a *good* Bible woman, *bad*.

More inquirers this year than ever before; numbers added are not yet so large but better than for some years. Many inquirers stop just short of a definite acceptance of Christ as Master. School teachers very indifferently recognize Christianity as the best religion, though a some go farther. Prejudices among *Shogakko* teachers are breaking up somewhat, a few Christian Normal school teachers doubtless helping here. Meetings are crowded, Christians earnest and active. At some other places few attend, there are no inquirers and no immediate prospects.

We had Taikyo Dendo only in Moji, Kokura and Wakamatsu. All Missions united, many scripture portion and tracts were sold and distributed. In Kokura results were small, more results at Wakamatsu, while at Moji meetings were crowded and many names handed in, the work going on under the Shimonoseki pastor. In Yamaguchi the work was simply an *enzetsukwai* (lecture meeting). Dr. Torrey's work brought in a large number of names, but the Y. M. C. A. being to the front it seemed necessary to wait for them and so the critical time was lost; many addresses of names handed in were false, many were already in Bible classes, others had lost their interest; still, some were hunted up and found Christ though not those who gave in their names. Some backsliding Christians have been stirred up to return, a good tendency noticeable everywhere at present. The Christians were roused to direct work, and his spirit is the best good to us from the Taikyo Dendo."

Miss PALMER, YAMAGUCHI, is also in evangelistic work but was somewhat interrupted by school work owing to Miss Bigelow's ill health:

"Though desiring to be away in outstations as much as possible, she finds that preparation and needed rest consume about half the time. a fact that ladies in country work will understand: a Japanese hotel, spending night and day on *tatami* (mats), the women visited thinking it inhospitable to leave one alone. Such cordiality does indeed warm one's own heart, still body and mind too are affected and so rest is needed. This much gives the reason for not working at times.

In these periods at home I visit and also teach a number of women in their own homes.

A meeting is held at each place every visit, but the quiet work in homes seems best; often Christians have inquiring friends willing to receive the foreigner. These quiet talks bring us nearer to each other. For gathering the women for Bible study and prayer my visits seem necessary, as, except where there is a strong nucleus, they are apt to get careless, though they are eager to meet with the missionary.

Briefly, 1st the dull condition one finds himself in at the close of a week means only that the body seeks to regain its poise after prolonged doubling, and the brain to overcome the strain of working backwards in the Japanese language for so long, 2nd, calling in homes for personal talks is more telling and lasting than formal gatherings, 3rd, visiting outstations as frequently as possible to encourage women to see the importance of woman's work for woman is desirable."

Mr. BROKAW, HIROSHIMA:—"There is no startling change due to Taikyo Dendo, rather there continue a deadly indifference to the gospel, a mad commercial and pleasure-seeking spirit, and persecution that often becomes active when one takes a stand for Christ, resulting in loss of position, family ostracism, &c. Still there is no rowdy opposition, but a sustained spirit of inquiry to know what the gospel is and can give. We have had a few baptisms, but nothing to justify the optimism about Japan in the home paper. Other places may justify this, but I fear the home church has been led on to a too lively hope.

My work is entirely evangelistic,—visiting outstations, touring, teaching classes and individuals, preaching wherever there is opportunity. Meetings are well attended being well advertised. Evangelists seem more hopeful and earnest as a result of Taikyo Dendo, and get hold of more inquirers. There are good S. schools at each outstation and Bibles are put on sale, and many are sold by evangelists. I made 5 carefully planned trips in connection with our Tsushin Dendo, (Correspondence Evangelism), tracts were sent ahead and scattered liberally, Bible portions were sold,—all making these trips the most effective in getting hearers. We still use the Fukuin Yako sending it to about 150. It has stirred up one here one there out of darkness into light on to baptism even.

Mrs. Brokaw and I teach Bible classes in our home, more and more with English left out. Mrs. Brokaw and Miss Nivling have done much in work among women. Miss Nivling (now Mrs. Madeley) has greatly improved the children's work of the S. school, has held in S. school a teacher's meeting, and conducted with Mrs. Brokaw meetings for women and children. They have done much visiting in homes making these visits more effective by Bible reading and prayer, and turning conversation towards the gospel."

MR. DOUGHTY, HIROSHIMA:—"My work covering the outstations of Iwakuni and Kure besides Hiroshima, is more prosperous now when I am unfortunately compelled to leave it than it has been since I came here. Baptized 8 persons at Iwakuni, meetings are crowded, S. school had to be divided, part meeting in the morning and part in the afternoon. The presbyterial evangelists and also Mr. Kiyama's meetings were singularly successful. At the present rate, we should have an organized church here in a year. The people talk of buying a place for a church. Their evangelist is an enthusiast on self-support.

In Kure, during 3 years and with a pastor not a single baptism took place. Last Fall I located a *kogisho* and evangelist there, giving the church also part of his time for part payment. The plan is not ideal but good, 2 were baptized and several more are to come. I taught a good Bible class there every week.

In Hiroshima I taught a Bible class of church members in church, also one twice a week at my home for non-Christians,—bank clerks school teachers, army officers,—leading to one baptism and more in prospect.

One main line of work has been teaching Christianity by correspondence, a plan conceived on my furlough. It consists in putting an advertisement in the daily paper, offering to send Christian literature free to any who wish to investigate. Making the method a real success is very hard work however. Still after 2 years I have great faith in it as a method of reaching forth into the interior, and it has given me the best satisfaction of all my work. A number have been baptized as a result and more are in prospect. In this connection I have published the Fukuin Geppo, a monthly of 8 pages for $2\frac{1}{2}$ years now, which has a circulation of 600. This and the correspondence plan I have passed over to Mr. Brokaw who from experience believes heartily in it. Some others have tried the method and the Japanese here believe thoroughly in it. I have also been at work on a handbook of Christian Literature but my return compels me to abandon it after finishing about one third of it."

Mr. Winn, Osaka:—" There is a more hopeful outlook, though the Taikyo Dendo's hopes have not been fully realized in additions to churches. There is an increase in interest however. The people are more accessible and so many more hear than formerly. I have worked with a satisfaction that comes from assurance that the truth is advancing. I preach on Sabbath and week-days as opportunities occur.

I have made one change in methods of work, viz. in using English teaching as an attraction. Hearing how one missionary among students gave an English address and another followed in Japanese on the same theme, this method securing a houseful of students, I resolved, to make two men out of one as I am alone in my itinerating. So I gave first an English speech and then followed with the best interpretation I could make in Japanese; using this method in several places and on many occasions, it succeeded above my expectations and above any other method I know of in bringing out good audiences of students both in and outside of Osaka. So I now regularly use this in towns where there are Middle Schools,--so far only in preaching places, thus getting young men into contact with our preachers.

In Osaka the use of English in some form is of great value, and is used by every mission more or less. Of course this is not necessarily the best, still less the only plan,—it is simply one of the plans which Providence puts into our hands to reach the young, especially the student class, and as such at least increases the bountifulness of our sowing in hope of an enlarged reaping.

The Osaka churches growing from our Mission's work are in an encouraging condition with increa ing attendance. New seats thus needed in the North Church were presented by the young men there, nearly all of whom entered it in the past 3 years. A brick wall also greatly improves this church property. The South Church got a new pastor in June and so there is hope for new life and growth there, though the former incumbent of 10 years also did his work well.

In outstations too the work is much more promising reaching many more than last year, due largely to certain changes among workers. The better classes are at least disposed to listen, instead of disdaining as once they did. The conviction of a need which only Christianity can supply, is growing, though the rebellion against the moral requirements of Christ is as great as ever.

Because of these and other encouraging signs this year has been one of more than ordinary joy in our Master's service."

Mrs. WINN, OSAKA:—(This work has been largely noted under English classes, industrial work, S. schools, children's meetings, &c.)

"The young men who became Christian through our English Bible class have formed a Y.P.S.C.E. and are doing praiseworthy work. They gave a charity concert, clearing 170 yen for the sufferers of the Ashio mines. Their wives are getting interested too."

MR. CURTIS, YAMAGUCHI and KYOTO:—(Mr. Curtis moved from Yamaguchi to Kyoto, to take up the place left vacant by Dr. Alexander.)

1 "Yamaguchi,—All classes are favorable here except Buddhists whose business is to oppose. My work has been largely for students, soldiers and R. R. men. The Y. M. C. A. has greatly increased in numbers and in earnestness to win fellow students. A public meeting to reach the soldiers going to and from the barracks is held every Sunday afternoon. At the request of the station master of our nearest R. R. station, meetings for the station employees were held, half in English teaching and half in

teaching Christianity in Japanese. The desire to have the religious teaching first lest some should be called away too soon was encouraging. It is wonderful how many R. R. employees are Christian or inquirers,—being as a class open to Christian impressions. Itinerating along the line to work among them, stopping also at stations, would be time well spent. Bundles of tracts firmly bound together and left in the waiting rooms show good usage by their worn out condition. Even the district governer thus got interested enough to order several copies of the *Sankoryo*.

Last August I helped in a summer school in Yanai and abundant opportunities occurred to reach with the gospel, school teachers and students, giving a lecture a day on God, sin and salvation following the tenor of the *Sankoryo*.

Dr. Torrey's services in February did much to stir up and to demonstrate the power of the old gospel and its adaptability to Japan.

2 Kyoto,—One reason causing me to hesitate about going to Kyoto was a sense of the difficulty of following a man like Dr. Alexander. Though this feeling still remains, I find the way paved by his influence as well as that of Mr. Porter whom the Christians here revere most fully. This accounts for their cordial welcome to me,—not a word thus far to remind us that we are *foreign* missionaries. Great doors are open in this great city which seems beginning to give some heed to Christ's claims."

MISS HAWORTH, KYOTO:—(Uppermost in the reports from Kyoto is the sense of loss in Dr. Alexander's departure).

"When Miss Haworth arrived from Osaka, Dr. A. was on a country tour. His enfeebled health on his return was noticed with alarm. But he kept up his work so well that until the day he left Kyoto, February 12th, his feebleness was not fully realized. February 11th was planned for final arrangements for erecting a church building, a desire cherished by Mr. Porter who secured the site and now it was brought to this stage by Dr. A. When this memorable day (February 11th) came Dr. A. had gone, as the leader explained, to Osaka for rest. The church's surprise was great for who had ever seen their faithful teacher rest. When however all unexpectedly he appeared in their midst the change of feeling was a study ; he was urged to take the chair. After a short address and after hearing subscriptions amounting to over 600 yen, God's blessing was invoked. Then he announced the physician's verdict, namely, that his own labors in Japan were ended. A solemn stillness in a little while broken by prayers, then a parting salutation and benediction by Dr. A. gave a scene never to be forgotten, felt rather than described. The emotions, the prayers, the thanks to God for sparing him so long to Japan, the tributes of affection, the trust in their beloved *sensei* was a beautiful reward for self-effacing labor.

Dr. A's. loss to the field is inexpressible. Too long in the state of his health sole representative of the work in this station, bearing the burdens of six persons amid complex circumstances and pressing opportunities, the work has suffered more than is recognized."

Mr. Curtis too writes,—" I desire to give my testimony to the wide and deep influence of Dr. A. all through Sanyo as well as here in Kyoto and Osaka, Tokyo, &c. An instance here to illustrate. At our farewell meeting in Yamaguchi, I took the occasion to refer to Dr. A. to whose vacant post I had been assigned. Announcing that word from Honolulu just received stated that his health had so far improved as to enable him even to preach, they expressed their great joy audibly and visibly and felt that their prayers for his recovery had indeed been answered; (they had observed a day of prayer for his recovery).

The work of the W. Japan Mission esp. in the Sanyo district was largely organized and for many years superintended by this veteran missionary who by his sympathetic tact and untiring efforts won the respect, love and confidence of our Japanese brethren in a most unique manner." (This same spirit won the same feelings toward him from the Tokyo field where he gave of his best and ripest work for eight years; indeed in the church at large it is doubtful whether any better encomiums have been won by any missionary worker.) Miss Haworth continues:—" In Kyoto, he had charge of all the work, did much preaching in Japanese, attended regularly the foreign preaching service, sharing in its ministry and the prayermeeting, was first president of the foreign theological club (this is attended also by a few Japanese), was the founder of the foreign recreation club though not much able to attend. He had a class for Bible study at his house, was visited by Japanese for counsel, doing his daily tasks as if each might be his last, a free dispenser of his means where it was needed to do good or set an example, laying up for himself no treasures upon earth.

The work in Kyoto embraces the church, a preaching place, two kindergartens,—in the house of one of which the church meets and on the same lot it is also to raise its new building,—a fine Sunday school in which the kindergarten teachers give efficient aid, while many pupils come from the kindergarten. There is a Y. P. S. of boys and girls from 10 to 15, a work started by Mrs. Porter, a monthly meeting for women whose collections is called the selfdenial fund, and the amount realized by the girls of the Y. P. S. C. E. aggregating 60 yen during the year, go into the church building fund. A Bible woman also does good service here. Messrs. Aoki and Wada, two teachers of the Doshisha, the former also principal of the Doshisha Girls School, are active members of our church, and so ought to be Mr. Hino, a graduate of Union, who however is a Kumiai. He was a member of a New York Presb. Church for two years, in which time 'he was never spoken two inside that church.' Marrying one of our young ladies recently he transplanted her too.

The Hon. K. Kataoka, of well-known standing, recently elected President of the Doshisha, has also been invited to enter Kumiai connections, as well as the previously named Messrs. Aoki and Wada, the former of Princeton Seminary, and the latter of the Imperial University. One frequently meets in Kyoto members of our sister church who were at one time members of the Nihon Kirisuto Kyokwai and feels just here the force of the term *union* while trying to understand its spiritual significance,—our name *Nihon Kirisuto Kyokwai** being here perhaps more comprehensive than ordinarily, and so, readily observed while modesty forbids its frequent specific use.

The Nishijin Kindergarten also affords a preaching place and a S. school of 50—70 pupils.

A daily service by the Cong. Mission and slightly supported by our church, near the Kitano festival which lasted 50 days, has been a feature of Taikyo Dendo. This festival is in honor of Sugihara Michizane, a famous exile of 1000 years ago, and, visited by missionaries and Japanese Christians with multitudes of heathen, shows how hard it is to draw the line between good and bad, notably the bad according to repute. The Kyoto dances far famed for their picturesqueness have lured rich and poor, high and low, pagan and Christian more than usual.

---

* Formerly *Itchi Kyokwai*, i e. United Church, a name still common.

To sum up:—A church small earnest but laboring under disadvantages. A desirable preaching place in a district scarce of laborers. Two Sunday schools claiming 150 pupils. Two kindergartens with an actual attendance of 80. Six Christian teachers all trained in mission schools and talented in different ways. An old Bible woman who has brought many to church in spite of her imperfections, and not ashamed of her calling. A Bible assistant and kindergartner who is a constant comfort because of her sensitive conscience, faith and fidelity. 100 homes actually open to Christian messengers without encroaching on other's grounds (careful consideration on this point is urged and heeded we believe.) A young men's class of Bible students. A woman's meeting of cheerful givers. A young people's society of 14 members ready to grow in numbers and interest. A cordial relation between the Japanese and foreigners.

The hospitality of the Cong. Mission long here before us should be gratefully acknowledged."

Mr. Fulton, Kanazawa:—Mr. Fulton reports for the evangelistic work, Mr. Dunlop reporting only on the work of the committee on girl's schools.

"Work is carried on as usual, in the same field and with the same workers. The result of Taikyo Dendo meetings for three weeks in union with the Methodists was 150 names of inquirers. Some of these still attend services and a few have been baptized. The movement advertised Christianity and gave Christians a new impetus. The Christians in the High School increased through it fourfold.

No baptisms outside of the city, but the popular attitude is more favorable. Correspondence Bible study continues to increase, nearly 400 being on the Kanazawa roll. This work touches points otherwise inaccessible and, is educational but needs personal contact for best results. This latter is difficult, and so the work is mostly seed sowing. Where we have personally touched, results are encouraging. Street preaching, book and tract-selling and visiting have yielded pleasant experiences.

In literary work I have furnished the Bible lesson for our semi-monthly "Yako." This is published with the help of Fukui and is now in its 5th year with a semi-monthly circulation of 1000 copies.

We work in unity and harmony with the Canadian Methodists but are unable to secure the co-operation of the Episcopalians. They persist in standing aloof from every undertaking that might be union and carry on their work entirely separately. We exceedingly regret this."

MISS LUTHER, KANAZAWA, also reports two S. Schools, a Sunday evening students' Bible class from the government schools showing great interest, some coming in advance for a prayer service praying for the newer members and for faith in God's word.

"Thus, for the children in schools, for the women in meetings, the young men students of the English Bible, the Sunday school, and the girls in our Girls School in daily Bible study, we endeavor to teach and show our love for Christ and pray that souls may be brought into his kingdom."

MR. JONES, FUKUI:—Heathenism and its concomitants continue here as opponents. No abatement is perceptible. Temples are going up. Towns are leaguing to refuse places for Christian meetings. Christians from elsewhere and inquirers are thus unwilling to identify themselves with Christians fearing the loss of temporal advantages. Inquirers do not desire us to come to their homes lest persecution come, several being threatened with expulsion from home if baptized. All this shows the hold of idolatry here yet.

Through our evangelist's sickness for 4 months and his work thus falling to me, I was prevented from doing all planned outside of Fukui. Two evangelists now give us better chances. We pay regular visits to 4 places and occasional ones to other points.

Although the city was greatly demoralized by the terrible fire on Easter, still the audience is increasing, and our prayermeetigs are exceptionally good. Our members being mainly young men we organized a Y. M. C. A. with semimonthly meetings. Five baptism and a number of inquirers are part of the year's results.

We too try to combine tract and Scripture selling with street preaching. For such bigoted antagonism as here this method is well adapted to disarm prejudice and to catch the ears of some not otherwise accessible.

We united in Taikyo Dendo meetings and a number signified their desire to study Christianity but beyond a broader sowing of the seed and the aroused activity of the Christians, no special results are so far perceptible."

MRS. JONES too speaks of the activity of genuine idolatrous heathenism whose devotees mostly illiterate, flock as pilgrims to temples here and there, being especially favored by cut R. R. rates to Kyoto; also of the unabated opposition of school teachers. Still she and her helpers have kept up gratifying work in Fukui and four big towns outside.

"In Sakae, 15 to 20 boys come. Behaving badly, discipline is needed at times and my last attempt used only because something had to be done, proved most effective. Asking them what they would think of a foreigner who went to a temple to ask questions about Buddhism and then was very rude to the priests, the best boy said emphatically, "Baka da," (He's a fool.) I said, "Please apply the principle." They saw the point and have behaved like gentlemen since.

In Marnoka where on account of snow we had to abandon meetings for 3 mos., the attendance averages 80. 10 or 12 boys ran away from a special lecture because they did not want to miss our meeting. As to results—many children and some women have the way of salvation in their heads and some in their hearts no doubt. It is hard for us not to see full results but it means something that for 3 years some of the same children have heard the gospel regularly. Weather here must not frighten one. If papers are torn up on the road, one must not lose heart. Withholding them the next time is usually effective. Antichristian clubs need to be ignored only, taking courage rather that Satan finds active opposition necessary. Make boys who come to scoff, teachable even at the risk of nervous prostration. 10 or 12 normal school students come to learn Christian hymns and to study Christianity. They enjoy this thoroughly, and I believe that the echoes of these hymns in their hearts will lead some to Jesus. There are 3 earnest inquirers now.

I have also a small class in the English Bible using Japanese explanations.

Calling is not much encouraged as women are more ready to come to the *kogisho* than to have their neighbors know that they have relations with the foreign teachers. Even the governors wife did not return my call, her husband being, it is said, afraid of Buddhist sentiment.

Rejoicing in the good news from other parts, we hope the time is near when even in the Hokurikudo there will be a great outpouring of God's awakening power."

North Japan Mission of the R. C. A.

Stations:—Yokohama, Tokyo, Nagano, Morioka, Aomori.

Rev. J. H. Ballagh, Yokohama:—Until the recent removal of Mr. Miller from Morioka to Tokyo, Mr. Ballagh, the oldest in the service of our number be it remembered, was the only one of this Mission in evangelistic work in this great center of Tokyo and vicinity. Inasmuch as the other Mission of our body in this general field is not overwell supplied with evangelistic workers (only 2 men's time being fully thus available, one of these being the veteran of the E. J. Pres. Mission and next to Mr. Ballagh in length of service among us, and as the field covered by these workers runs from Shizuoka to Yokohama, across the bay to Boshu, Chiba, and north west through Gumma, Shinshiu and on past Niigata (Mr. Scudder however being in this region and reaching south to Matsumoto and Iida) our Council seems hardly ready to plead guilty to the charge of throwing itself away on a missionary congested center. In fact the 10 millions or so in this field might perhaps give work to a few more missionaries from that body which by right of priority and strength in numbers and church membership ought not to yield the palm in the center too easily. But to the report from our veteran of 40 years,—

" Places where stated workers in Shizuoka Ken are found are Shizuoka, Mishima, Ishiimura, Koyama and Gotemba. No marked advance is discernible a few baptisms having been administered by Rev. Miura and Rev. Ito. Mr. Ito for several years self-supporting, doing Christian work at Yokohama, and elsewhere, reentered the Mission's service. Owing to the exaggerated teaching by a former lay worker Sakuma Matsunosuke about the Lord's coming, a Japanese Dowie without Chicago connection however, there was a defection at Mishima, Koyama and Gotemba. About 50 had resigned from connection with Presbytery, but many are disillusioned again and affiliate with the N. K. K. believers there now under Mr. Ito's care. Mr. Date, evangelist at Ishiimura, owing to sickness moved to Mishima and helps now at Gotemba though not fully recovered. Another worker at Mishima also supplies Kashiwakubo, Hakone, Yamanaka, and one or two other places. At Iwamoto is a worker under the Woman's Union Mission, while at Suzukawa is an independent worker under Mr. Ito's or my oversight. The priests tried to frighten away the large number of pupils whom this last worker once a notorious priest, had trained in Christian doctrine.

At Yokohama the Mission has our Ota chapel with regular services of which first Mr. Ito and then Mr. Harasawa until his removal to Tokyo, acted as pastor.

In Boshin Mr. Yoshioka after visiting the field located at Oyamamura and works also at Oknyamamura. At Hojo and Tateyama a seminary student works during the summer, the leading believers there desiring to share in the choice and support of the workers, being hard to please. Visits have been made to these and various other places. At Okubo 6 were baptized, results of work of Bible women of the Womans Union Mission,—a bright spot in Chiba ken. A dark spot was the suicide of one who seemed a very hopeful believer at Oyamamura.

North of Tokyo, a division in the Wado region resulted in all being cut off from Presbytery, except Kasukabe,—a deplorable result. Thus the Mission rule not to extend help outside the N. K. K., cuts off a scant allowance of a helper here, a result to be regretted as the work otherwise is growing and satisfactory.

North Shinshin or the Nagano field is under Mr. Scudder's care. In South Shinshin, Mr. Maki is striving hard to strengthen the work at Matsumoto, giving also 10 hrs. to English in the Middle School to interest the students in the Gospel. Good results may come from some lecture meetings. Suwa, Sakashita and Iida have each had an evangelist, though one of then recently left to work under Mr. Hope of Toyohashi. Signs of advance are seen, and each place is striving for a church building.

In general the people are more ready to listen, and there is less need of apologetics and more of direct evangelistic effort. A time of a people prepared by God to hear his Gospel is upon us. O, for a hundred fold more laborers and for a vast increase of faith in the proclamation of the gospel!"

MR. BOOTH, YOKOHAMA in addition to his administration of Ferris Seminary, reports himself as theo. faculty of the Bible course, and pastor of Union church, adding.

"This is not the place to report but it may not be out of place to say that the Sunday afternoon Bible class for European young men continues and is attended by from 12 to 20, and that the work done among and for young men by the Brotherhood of Andrew and Philip gives promise of good results. The Y. P. S. C. E. has carried on a unique work through their missionary committee. They secure sustaining members for the employment of the field secretary and not only distribute copies of the Endeavor " but also manitain through cooperation with the Japanese city pastors, a service on Sunday afternoons for domestics in the service of the foreigners. The committee would like to secure an evangelist who is fit for this needed work. Recommendations are in order.

MR. MILLER, MORIOKA and TOKYO:—This report gives considerable details of the Taikyo Dendo movement in north Japan. This was begun by sending a choir along with the speakers on a tour among towns in the vicinity of Sendai. This new venture produced such satisfactory results that the choir was adopted as part of the regular country services. Three of this choir were young men of various Sendai schools. In Morioka a large hall was used for meetings, afternoon meetings being specially held for students. Country places visited by these bands are Hanamaki, Mizusawa, Ichinoseki and others. At Hanamaki alone an earnest Buddhist attempted to foment a disturbance. Dr. Harris a former Methodist missionary in Japan, now working among the Japanese in San Francisco, did good service on a tour through northern Japan at this time. Old Father Okuno had for years desired to make a tour all over Japan to preach the gospel; now with some funds for traveling expenses from America he was at length able to carry out his long cherished plan, first in the center and south in 1900 and in 1901 in the north, accompanied by a devoted helper Mr. H. Sato, who had labored long at Yokosuka. In Morioka the manner of attracting the people to the meetings was a crude imitation of Tokyo methods,—(for a succinct account of Tokyo methods see Dr. Imbrie's statement in last year's Council Report); struggling bands went around the streets with lanterns and banners, one young man ringing a dinner bell and another making a doleful noise on an accordion on which he could not play a tune.

In company with Mr. Pierson, Mr. Miller made a tour of the Hokkaido lecturing at Kushiro and villages along the coast as far as Otsu, then at Moiwa, and Obihiro. At all there places the main work is in the hands of the C. M. S. Then on to Kamikawa as far as Asahigawa, where Mr. Pierson lives.

The scattered towns and villages of the Hokkaido can in summer be agreeably reached on foot or on packhorses provided at the post stations and amid novel if not agreeable incidents often. The people are open to Christian teaching and ready to identify themselves with Christians, some of whom can be found in almost every place, or at least such as have enjoyed Christian teaching.

To the meetings held for the past two years by the Sendai Ger. Ref. Mission for the spiritual and intellectual benefit of their evangelists, our own workers are welcomed receiving much profit.

The autumn manœuvres afforded an opportunity to reach many of the soldiers, esp. through two tracts written for soldiers at the time of the Chino-Japan war, which being out of print Mr. Miller had struck off anew.

In connection with Mr. Miyama, the temperance lecturer, we took occasion to reestablish work it Noheji after an interval of rest. I accompanied him in meetings at Morioka, Hanamaki, Mizusawa and Ichinoseki.

Thus more evangelistic work has been carried on in this northern field than before. Results in baptisms will belong rather to the new year however.

In Aomori a parsonage has been built.

MR. AND MRS. MILLER's removal to Tokyo in April and Mr. and Mrs. Harris's return from furlough thither have been noted. At last accounts a further change is impending, Mr. and Mrs. Harris taking up again the work they left in Aomori while the Misses Winn and Deyo occupy Morioka.

MR. MILLER's work in Morioka extended from 1888 to March, 1902. The record of the Morioka kogisho during this period is as follows:—

Baptisms	158
Received by letter and confirmation. . .	48
Total . . .	206
Dismissed by letter . .	52
Dropped from roll . .	9
Died	8
Excluded	1
Total .	70
Suspended .	3

Present on roll in Morioka . . 136
Absent from ,, . . . 70
Total 206

Mrs. MILLER has as usual the editing of the two semimonthlies *Glad Tidings and Little Tidings* with issues of 3100 and 4300 copies respectively. Besides this she paid weekly visits to two hospitals in Morioka, kept up the women's meetings, and the singing in a S. school averaging over 70 pupils.

Mr. SCUDDER NAGANO:—"We have not been able to persuade our people to follow Taikyo Dendo methods farther than to adapt the Sunday evening service more for non-church goers, preceding it with a half hour song service, and an occasional magic lantern talk. On S. afternoons our young men several times called on about 400 houses leaving printed advertisements of our meetings, a tract and extending invitations. The evening audiences have thus been trebled and the meetings are far more spirited. Besides the English Bible class the S. School work and the singing class already referred to, a special class for inquirers and Bible study among Normal School students has been held. From the work of Messrs. Helm and Takai last April when the attendance of students reached 200, we hope for good results. From Christian literature sent by mail favorable reports have come in."

Mr. HARRIS (MORIOKA) says in a private letter,—"I find plenty to do in to do this field. I started off with a Bible class of 8 young men from the Normal and High Schools. Last Sunday it numbered 70. The body of the church is packed full. It is a class of young men I want to get hold of and for three Sundays I have given it to them straight."

MISS WINN, AOMORI:—"Our little church has passed through various and trying vicissitudes during the past year. We now have a recent graduate of the M. G. Theo. Dept. who succeeds in drawing the young men. Besides 3 S. schools in the city we have work in two outside places. At Noheji we have an inquirer who seems taught of the Holy Spirit. Though poor and not yet baptized he opens his house for meetings refusing remuneration with the remark that he considers it an honor and a privilege to have the Gospel preached in his house. A number of Bibles have been sold, one man coming 12 *ri* to buy one, being first interested by a tract on temperance. Everywhere people seem ready to hear, and we cannot utilize all our opportunities."

MISS WYCKOFF spent part of her energy in Aomori, and part in Ferris Seminary, to the Bible school department of which it is reported she has been assigned altogether now. In her report she gives interesting details of the Taikyo Dendo work as connected with the pupils of Ferris Seminary. One incident alone can be given here. In one of the upper classes all but two were Christians. For months the rest had been praying for these two, each girl going daily after dinner to pray alone and once a month in concert for them. The Taikyo Dendo was an occasion to be specially utilized, and so they invited these two to the meetings, promising to call on their way. Soon one of them announced her decision to be a Christian. Long before she and the other non-Christian girl had mutually agreed never to become Christians, an agreement she now at length found she could live up to no longer. So renouncing her promise she gave herself up to Christ.

Classes in English of Normal School girls and young men were held, to which a short Bible lesson was attached, the young men coming also on Sunday to church and at their own request to a Bible class on Sunday afternoons, 40 of these students attended special evangelistic services. Work in two S. schools formed a further field of labor.

MISSION OF THE REFORMED (GERMAN) CHURCH IN THE U. S.

DR. SCHNEDER writes:—In evangelistic work the past year has been an encouraging one. Though on account of my duties in Sendai I have not been able to visit our country stations much, whenever I did have time to go I have seen evidences of growing interest. At some of our places there has been much activity; at others more quiet growth; a few have simply held their own, most doing more.

MR. MILLER, H. K., SENDAI:—"Our work has joined in the 20th Century movement. 2 campaigns were organized and a great deal of preaching done. The audiences were large and deeply interested. Direct appeals to repent and believe, or at least to inquire into Christ's claims were made. God's Spirit is no doubt striving with men's hearts here and the attitude to the gospel has greatly improved.

Mr. Mott's brief visit affected us as well as Tokyo favorably, a number of students becoming inquirers, some having since been received into the church.

We are confronted with difficulties in manning our work. A few of the Japanese evangelists are restless, eager to go to America or to start some new work, and so it is hard for such to devote themselves completely and steadily to building up selfsupporting churches. Others soon wear out in a given place and must be transferred frequently. Still there are some whose quiet patient and persevering work deserves at least commendation. Five or six of the teachers of the Tohoku Gakuin have given much valuable help in evangelistic work without pay except traveling expenses. Several students too are thus employed, and this enables them to pursue their studies while gaing experience and giving aid in the work.

With a few exceptions there is but little effort in the direction of selfsupport. Workers take little more than a theoretical interest in this matter and circumstances are such as not to make it necessary or even expedient for them to educate their people in this duty. The workers too are mostly of a dependent spirit or feel diffident about asking people to pay towards their own salary."

The rules and regulations of the evangelistic committee of this Mission are here subjoined.

Revised Rules and Regulations of the Evangelistic Committee.

(Adopted Mar. 27 1902.)

1 All salaries and allowances for *dendōhi* (travel) and current expenses shall be paid on the fifteenth of the month.

2 If a newly appointed evangelist arrives at his station before the fifteenth of the month, he shall be entitled to a full month's salary; if after the fifteenth, only one-half shall be paid.

3 All evangelists are required to submit monthly reports to the respective missionaries in charge, according to forms supplied by the Committee.

4 Allowances for moving, travel or current expenses are made for the purpose of defraying the actual and legitimate, (not estimated,) expenses incurred. Whenever money is advanced, a detailed account must be rendered to the missionary in charge, and any balance remaining must be returned through him to the treasurer.

5 Unless otherwise specified, the allowances for moving and *dendōhi* are made on the basis of third class railroad tickets.

6 No evangelist may leave his station for a week or more without the permission of the missionary in charge.

The Committee also took the following action:

"*Resolved* that, for the purpose of developing the spirit of self-support, the Evangelistic Committee pursue the following policy in the case of Kanda (Tokyo) church, Iwanuma church, Ishinomaki church, and Nakamura, Haranomachi, Shiroishi and Tome *kōgisho*, the time of its actual execution to be left to the discretion of the missionary in charge:

(a) That the Committee help the *kōgisho* (or church) directly, rather than the evangelist in charge;

(b) That all financial help be paid into the treasury of the *kōgisho* (or church);

(c) That the *kōgisho* (or church), subject to the approval of the missionary in charge, be empowered to call its own evangelist, fix his salary and accept his resignation."

The statistics of this Mission for 1900 and 1901 (in totals) are as follows:

	1900	1901
Ordained ministers.	8	10
Unordained evangelists.	28	25
Church buildings.	17	18
Meeting places.	44	38
Membership communicants).	2003	2142
Baptized children.	114	128
Adult baptisms.	123	269
Infant baptisms.	5	41
Total additions.	183	335
Total losses.	138	151
Sunday schools.	40	40
„ „ scholars.	1223	1420
Total expenditures.	¥ 12234.020	¥ 15532.619
Contributions by Japanese.	4685.880	5139.372

Mr. Noss, Sendai:—"While doing heavy work in school, and having charge of a chapel in Sendai and stations in south Miyagi, I have devoted all spare time to the Eng. edition of Lange's Textbook of Colloquial Japanese, translating it from the German and now more than half completed.

In evangelistic work Fukushima Ken is most promising and Yamagata Ken most backward. More help and supervision from headquarters is greatly needed. Our Mission is too weak to do all this for its evangelists. Thus also outside of Sendai Taikyo Dendo has not had much direct influence. To me the most encouraging feature is the renewed sense of responsibility shown by laymen in the church.

By means of our Tohoku Kyokwai Jiho we hope to create an appetite for the Fukuin Shinpo. The evangelists reading club continues successfully." Following is a copy of its rules:

Regulations of the Tōhoku Ministerial Reading Club.

1 The order of the stations is determined by the Secretary. When it is necessary to change the order, the Secretary will instruct those concerned.

2 Periodicals must be forwarded to the next member on the 15th and at the end of every month. Books shall be forwarded at the end of every month. If the day falls on a Sunday they shall be sent the next day. For every day's delay a fine of one *sen* will be imposed. A parcel may be sent before the appointed time, but in that case the next member gets the benefit of the extra time.

3 When a member has to leave his station temporarily, so that there is no one there to receive parcels, he must inform the member from whom he usually receives them. If he does not, he is responsible for the waste of postage incurred.

4 When a member leaves his station permanently he must send all books and periodicals to the next station and report to the Secretary, who will make proper arrangements.

5 Each member is required to send in monthly reports according to forms provided by the Club.

6 The regular dues are twenty-five *sen* a month, or three *yen* a year.

7 Dues will be collected on the 15th of December every year, adding the fines. The amount expended for postage, etc., as reported from month to month, will be subtracted. Expenditures not so reported cannot be refunded.

Mr. SNYDER SENDAI:—"This year my work has been very largely, with the *Bible cart.* For years I believed that by using a cart many Scriptures could be sold. Now I have tried it and proved it.

Last September with a student for a helper I began work north of

Sendai. We had a nice little cart with banners flying above. We pulled it from town to town and going through each street we sold to those who come out to see what it was and also called at the houses on either side. In this way hardly a house was missed and thousands read the Word of God for the first time.

We would always ask the evangelists and Christians to help. Thus we sometimes had quite a large body of workers.

In Tokyo during the holiday season I used a stand and also a cart part of the time with the usual results. About the middle of January I started for Kyushu for a 100 days trip. I regularly had two Japanese helpers with me, using the cart. Local workers, missionaries, pastors, Bible women, etc., were always asked to help and in many places rendered most valuable assistance.

We touched at all the large cities except Nagasaki also at many smaller ones. In the smaller places we sold more books in proportion to the number of houses than in the cities. One great reason of this is the fact that in the cities more have already purchased them and have an opportunity to buy any day they wish.

The great willingness to buy makes we wish that the whole of Japan could be covered, a call being made at each house, at least once in two years, for when one calls the person who would gladly buy may not be at home, also people change their notions, and in general there is quite a change in most homes in two years especially where small children are growing up.

Our main effort has been to sell the single gospels, but not neglecting the Testaments or full Bibles which we always carried with us. We found those who had previously bought portions were now ready for a Testament.

One man who bought three portions last year told us that they had led him to repent and he is now a member of the Nihon Kirisuto Kyokwai at Moji.

One who bought from me in Tokyo was influenced to go to an evangelistic meeting that evening and is an earnest inquirer. Another who bought on perhaps the same day went to the same church and is now a member thereof. Such instances encourage us to do all in our power to sow the seed,—" the seed is the word of God."

In a year I have sold over 70000 copies including 125 Bibles and 2580 Testaments. In the three years during which I have been devoting most of my time to this work the total is 184795 including 4767 Testaments and 337 Bibles.

If the willingness, yes, readiness of the people to investigate and study Christianity is a favorable condition, we certainly are laboring at a time when the opportunities are very great. May God bless His own Word."

Mr. LAMPE, SENDAI,—has (1) been teaching in both departments of the Tohoku Gakuin, (2) has had charge of a good part of the Missions business matters, acting as treasurer and also building a house, (3) in evangelistic work has just begun to preach in Japanese. As a result of Bible class teaching 7 policemen were baptized last year, and further work led to the baptism of 6 more a short while ago,—13 of the best policemen of the Ken,-these in turn endeavoring to bring others to Christ. (4) Language study owing to these other duties has been sadly interfered with, though convinced that a missionary's usefulness depends largely op n his knowledge of the language.

Mr. FAUST, SENDAI,—Since I wrote my last report to the Council of Missions the All-wise Father saw fit to call to the eternal home above, my faithful and devoted help-meet and wife. The bereavement is most grievous and bitter but His comforting grace is sufficient for me even in this extremity. I have resigned myself to His leading and have relied wholly upon His love and He has strengthened me and has not forsaken me. His will be done.

Teaching in the Tohoku Gakuin, both depts., S. school work, preaching or evangelistic work and language study constitute my work. On an evangelistic trip to Yamagata 7 person were baptized. The number of baptisms in our field during the year was larger than that of any previous year in the history of our work (a remark that probably applies to the church as a whole).

I am overseer of a S. school in Nagamachi with teachers from our boys' and girls' schools. Here also an evangelist is located and the women's meetings are good. Four of my Eng. Bible class received baptism.

EAST JAPAN MISSION OF THE PRESBYTERIAN CHURCH (NORTH.)

STATIONS:—Tokyo, Yokohama, Sapporo, Otaru, Asahigawa.

Special mention should be made of a visit from Miss Ellen Parsons, editor of Woman's Work for Woman, who on a tour of missions around the world also visited this Mission the latter part of June.

Dr. Thompson, Tokyo:—" Evangelistic work under my general supervision has been carried on during the past year at Meisei church and Tsunohadzu in Tokyo, and at Hachioji, Urawa, Gyoda, Kirin, Omata, Ashikaga and Utsunomiya in the country. Rev. Y. Ogawa gives nearly all his time to Meisei Church. Rev. Mr. Fukuda has labored chiefly at Tsunohadzu and Hachioji. Mr. Akasu is stationed at Urawa, and looks after work at Gyoda. From lack of qualified preachers and the means to support them in their work the other places mentioned above have all been left to take care of themselves, being only occasionally visited at irregular intervals. Under such circumstances it is entirely too much to expect that Christian work will prosper at any time, much less when it is hindered, as is sometimes the case, by quarrels and scandals. However even the worst cases in my field have not yet gone so far that they need be despaired of or abandoned, and at some the outlook is decidedly hopeful. At Kirin a convenient church building has been erected by the people without mission aid. The same is true of Tsunohadzu, where a neat church edifice has been built by the foreign and Japanese friends of the late Mrs. True to her memory. There is also a small church building at Omata, and one, the Meisei church, in the city. At all the other points services are held in rented rooms or private houses. Besides the general supervision of evangelistic work in this wide field and some care for the Tsunohadzu Sanatorium and Training School for nurses, I have quite recently taken part in the late Taikyo Dendo or Forward Movement in Kyobashi-ku. Compared with the same work of last year the meetings in the several churches were perhaps not o will attended, and were a trifle less enthusiastic, and there was less urging the hearers to come to a decision, still there was throughout unusual interest manifested. The main features of the compaign that has just ended in Kyobashi-ku were much the same as last year, namely, a central prayer meeting every day at 3 p.m. with preaching services every night for eight days, in seven different churches. The churches taking part this year were the Church Christ in Japan, the M. E. church, the Evangelical Association, the Independent Pres. (Mr. Tamura's church), the United Brethren and the Baptist Churches. These were reinforced and materially aided by a volunteer band of street-heralds organized recently in Tokyo by foreigners and Japanese trained in Mr. Moody's school, Chicago. These with their musical instruments and particular methods are very helpful at such a time. They will doubtless yet aid this work in other wards of the city, and throughout the country. About 700 attended each night; a hundred or more at each preaching place. Nearly 400 expressed a desire to receive further instruction, and half as many declared their resolution to live a Christian life. Many things conspire to make this work look promising. The audiences were composed of mature men and women from the vicinity of each preaching place. They listened quietly till the end. Few went out during the services. There were fewer young men and boys. They apparently begin to feel that they may freely enter our churches. Harmony prevailed. The young men and women of the churches showed not only willingness but eagerness to engage in the work; the prayers were earnest, and the discourses, one and all, were sound, evangelical and practical, every way adapted to the class of hearers addressed. Different methods of further prosecuting the work and conserving the results will be tried. The M. E. Church intends, I understand, to try to gather in the inquirers in family or household prayer-meetings held in the vicinity. Shinsakai Church (Pres) has resolved to gather its inquirers into a Sat. evening Bible class for fuller instruction. Other methods may be resorted to in other churches. But whatever the method, doors for activity and usefulness will be opened up which were formerly closed or non-existent. This is a consideration which should lead us to value this Taikyo Dendo work. The methods hitherto pursued may be continued; or being flexible, may be readily changed to suit altered circumstances. There would be no difficulty in one church carrying it on alone, or in two or three neighboring churches uniting in it; or in all the churches joining in a general onward movement. All this makes the outlook appear promising. By the prosecution of the work as it has been begun the gospel may soon be *heralded* at least to all the land. The attention of all may be thus arrested quickly. Afterwards, or at the same time, men of mature learning, wisdom and wealth should exert themselves to plant permanent Christian institutions, churches, schools and charitable establishments as lights at suitable points throughout the land, or as places of refuge for those, who if Taikyo Dendo *only* is carried on, are in danger of being left as sheep without a shepherd."

Mr. MacNair in additions to excerpts already made on various lines of work reports that his evangelistic work is the same as formerly, consisting of preaching at stated intervals in certain of the Tokyo churches and in those of Chiba province.

Miss YOUNGMAN gives her time to evangelistic work comprising two stations in Tokyo known as the Ueno and Kamejima missions, and the work in Kamakura, besides other lines, such as Bible classes, women's and children's meetings, work connected with the *Kozensha* and the Leper Hospital on the southern borders of Tokyo. "Last year at this hospital a chapel was built, and now a house for the women is being erected. Eleven were baptized here recently leaving only 6 out of the 40 still out of Christ. Miss Parsons, editor, of the Woman's Work for Woman, visiting the hospital remarked that she had been around the world and had seen many homes for lepers but that this was the cleanest and brightest one she had visited, also that the sight of ten lepers baptized was a sight of a lifetime, most impressive. Having undertaken this work without any experience or even knowledge of its needs, it was very encouraging to us all to have it thus spoken of. Though we have a faithful corps of workers, still there is so much that is depressing and difficult in this work and we are tried beyond measure sometimes. Financially we have received all we asked for and our hands were accordingly full with buying land and building houses; but all this also increases labor and responsibility. We never have room for all that apply. In fact many more would apply if they dared, but applying to us means registering their names as lepers and this brings their families into disrepute. A leper woman is now wandering about Yokohama. She was four years in the Catholic hospital at Koyama. She was required to register and she said she could not do it as her sister was happily married and had two little children; she feared that if her sister's husband knew that she had a leper sister he would send away both mother and children. One man went to his home to get his registration papers and he was shut up in the day-time by his brothers who had reported him dead and when at night they talked with him and he told them he would stay till he got his papers, they told him if he did not go back to Tokyo, they would kill him. He came back however and received his papers shortly after.

The government is looking into the matter of leprosy and it reports over 30000 lepers in Japan, though there would be doubtless twice that number if the hidden ones could be found and added. When we opened this place, we built a house for contagious diseases, but in 8 years we have not had a case of contagion on hand. In this and many other special ways God has shown his loving care of us.

The Kamejima mission received a great impetus by being moved to another section of the city though 2½ months were lost through the red tape required to make the change.

Statistics as follows:—

Attendance at daily prayermeetings		1585
„	„ preaching	3675
„	Bible class	457
„	Sabbath school	911
„	children's meetings	917
„	women's meetings	357
„	magic lantern lectures	121
		8023

Tracts, distributed 1060, offerings of C. E. Society 8.50 of which used 2.00 to help an old woman, 4.50 for poor schoolars and 2.00 for Okayama orphans.

The Ueno mission is now in its 13th year of daily and nightly work. The open air services in the Park reach hundreds every Sabbath who might never enter a church. Although since Mr. Waddell's depaiture no foreigner has been regularly preaching there, there has been no falling off in the number of hearers. Statistics:—

Attendance at preaching in the *kogisho*.		6015
„	„ „ Park	11690
„	Bible class	412
„	prayer meetings	1628
„	children's meetings	1277
Visitors to the reading room		236
Attendance at women's meetings		151
„	inquirers, „	16
Baptized and united with church		12
Workers,—9 men and 3 women		12
Tracts distributed		3800
Inquirers at present		11
Adults reached		20148
Children „		1277
Total „		21425

The Kamakura work carried on by a Bible woman has reached over 3000. Thousands more might be reached through an evangelist and a tent that is on hand.

Mrs. McCAULEY, TOKYO:—"The Rescue Home for fallen women has claimed a portion of my time. And fruit has been realized; eight girls were led to a better life, and twelve little girls saved from being sold. Three of the girls of last year have during the year professed Christ and entered the church. One married a Christian man. Three girls from the Rescue Home are now trained nurses and doing well; all are Christians.

The Leper Home takes a little of my time. At a meeting on May 27th, 2 women came out on the Lord's side and asked for baptism. Ten are now among the inquirers.

The year has been indeed a harvest time. Souls have been garnered in and the beautiful growth in the workers has been a cause of deepest thanksgiving."

Miss Gardner with an experienced Bible woman carries on women's meetings in two Tokyo churches, and also conducts two Bible classes for young men which Miss Helena Wyckoff takes during her absence on furlough. Miss Ballagh's absence in made good is Tsunohazu by Mrs. Fukuda's earnest work for the children there. The new chapel, a memorial to Mrs. True, restores to them the home of which fire had deprived them a few years ago.

Along with one of her Bible women Miss Milliken works in Honjo church where many inquirers appeared as the fruit of Taikyo Dendo, and for whom she has special meetings, while the other Bible woman gives most of her time to the poor in Shinano Machi. Mrs. Milliken attends women's meetings in two churches, while her assistant has been cordially welcomed among the sick and poor. It is touching to see how those who have known little or nothing about Christianity turn to that as a door of hope when their path slopes down into the shady valley. Among them Dr. Imbrie's "A Door into Heaven" and "The Gospel of God" and a little tract, "Just a Word" have been found helpful.

We now turn to our evangelists of the far-north, the frozen north we might say, for last winter at least the record reached in that vicinity from 40° to 50° below zero.

Mr. Pierson's report is so condensed that to boil it down still further would overconcentrate it and make it indigestible to many perhaps.

I. Taikyo Dendo results:—"The year just past has been to me more full of cheer in our Hokkaido work than any of the past eight.

Taikyo Dendo has left us good results. Taikyo Dendo itself was a result of long prayer and preparing and we thank the Lord not only for the goal but for the course. Our churches have received new life. The Christians here in Asahigawa deliberately vote for a two hour service and sustain the interest so thoroughly that one seems almost selfish in taking his part. We can not state the case mathematically but the whole life of the Church has been quickened and the life is genuine; for the plans for the year's campaign may be summed up in this—*to teach the Bible*. There are four new candidates for the ministry in our field, two in the Mombetsu region and two in Asahigawa. These are seed bearing fruits.

Self support has during the year been quadrupled; so that now we can employ a new evangelist *with funds raised on the field*. So it comes to pass that before we have our much desired Presbytery, we have a local home mission committee in operation. For this we are especially grateful. Note in passing that while the Japanese church may not be abreast the Corean Church (and all honour to the Corean Church!) yet when all the various items in the list of contributions—to the central Home Board, gifts to pastors, special meeting funds, Taikyo Dendo collections, local charities and all are added together, they make no mean showing. One place has not contributed to "pastor's salary" (which is almost synonymous with "self support") yet it has built a church edifice and a pastor's house and is now addressing itself to raising the pastor's salary. The self support column does not contain all

II. New work presecuted in 1901.—Two miles out of Asahigawa lie the 7th Army Division Barracks. The road into town is lined with temptations. We secured a well located house and opened a Y. M. C. A. assembly room, reading-room and school. The whole work was put into the hands of the Y. M. C. A. which is composed of members of all our three churches. Every Sunday we have preaching for the soldiers who pass through this street in great numbers. The services have been most interesting. They hear the gospel. There are English classes for soldiers and officers three evenings a week, the Bible story being the subject taught. There is a fairly well furnished reading room, and adjoining this a school room where the twelve or so Ainu children are taught on week days as well as Sundays. Within a few yards of our building is an Ainu house and beyond there are 20 or 30 scattered houses that make up the Ainu village. We stand between the living and the dead: it is pitiful to see the race going.

During the year we have sold some Gospels mostly on the trains; the number seems to be fixed at about 60 to a train. The other day at a big festival we set up a little stand and sold only about half that number, but preached a whole series of sermons; no house rent, no lights and fuel, plenty of good ventilation and a congregation with an interest directly as your vocal endurance or the spiritual power you possess. The gospels make good texts and all the while you are preparing some one to *buy* that he may know more.

III. Our particular churches:—

We have now
{
two churches self supporting
two churches about ½ self supporting
two strong chapels ¼ self supporting
two strong chapels small in numbers and in the day of beginnings
two strong chapels in prospect not yet *in se*.
}

We cherish great hopes for the two strong chapels. We hope with God's blessing soon to see them churches and then our Hokkaido Presbytery!

We are nothing but comity up here in the Hokkaido; just read the account of our Hakodate Conference last summer. Exchange of pulpits, the C. M. S. cordially uniting in common in that city and we are growing together more and more. In Asahigawa we have *two* union prayer meetings a month, and occasionally exchange pulpits. Notice too in the report of Hakodate Conference the resolutions we passed about occupying new fields.

In conclusion we must bear our testimony, too, to these points:

1 Fidelity of our preachers and evangelists (who are living on low salaries, but) who are doing good service.

2 Sober thinking on the things of the soul we believe exists throughout our country districts especially.

3 The whiteness of the fields to *harvest*. Now is the day of our *reaping*.

4 Importance of a more aggressive work among the soldier farmer colonies and farmers in general. The country *district churches* ought to be strong churches.

With faith hope and good cheer."

Mrs. Pierson's report is not merely interesting and characteristic so that a mere brief of it would disappoint when the whole may be had, but it is also so suggestive of a missionary wife's life and a model of work that one has not the heart to attempt a condensation of it. Those who have read her paper on "How Best to Conserve Taikyo Dendo Results," in the Japan Evangelist of last winter need not be apprehensive either of vain repetitions. The following report is an original contribution and worthily closes our report on evangelistic work.

Mrs. G. P. Pierson:—"Our regular work at this station is almost purely evangelistic and may be summed up under the following ten heads:

1 *Receiving visitors:*—This takes up by far the greatest part of our time. During the year 1901, counting from January to January, we have received 968 callers, the majority of whom came to hear about "The Way," and all of them *did* hear it before they left. On one day we had 28 callers. They represent the various classes and conditions found in the Hokkaido, viz.:—Merchants, R. R. employes, officials, workmen, hotel-keepers, country school-teachers, soldiers, farmers, soldier-colonists, factory-girls, Buddhist and Shinto priests, Ainu, newspaper-editors, actors, owners of large nōjō (farms), colonists, carpenters, trades-people, detectives, police-men; the sick ask for bodily healing as one poor man who had seen a picture of Christ healing the man born blind, came to ask the "Jesus people" to heal his eyes; and the oppressed seek release at our hands. Of the 968 callers, 88 were Ainu men, women and children. The men usually come to be entertained or rarely to be taught; the women for medecine for their sick children, or to sell carved trays and trinkets or picturesque mats or garments of their own weaving and embroidery.

2 *Meetings:*—Besides these 968 callers, 1433 other people have attended the various meetings that have been held from time to time in our house during the year,—55 in all, such as womens' meetings, temperance meetings, united prayer-meetings, Taikyo Dendo meetings, Taikyo Dendo hymn practisings, magic lantern meetings, consecration and holiness meetings, church sociables, workers'

prayer meetings, a full-fledged Salvation Army meeting addressed by Adj. Hatcher of the S. A. and attended by 100 people, rescue-work meetings, regular church and Sunday school services (for a short time while our new Church was being built), knitting-classes, Christian Endeavour meetings, a debate meeting on Buddhism v. Christianity—publicly so advertised beforehand without our knowledge or consent, and carried on almost without either in our own house willy-nilly, by an enterprising Buddhist lecturer, who afterwards announced that he had had a 5 hours " *Toronkwai*" with the "foreign Jesus-teacher" and had beaten him at every point. Just this morning I learned that the Buddhist lecturer after arguing with Mr. Pierson for 5 hours publicly stated that when the "Jesus-teacher" saw him coming he got on his bicycle and rode away and stayed away for hours! 3 of our young men attended a Buddhist lecture, attempted to answer the man and got stoned going home. We had also children's meetings, young men's meetings and latterly old men's meetings.

3 *Calling and House'to House Visiting:*—That this matter of visiting is one of the very best evangelistic methods I am strongly convinced and regret that I have only made about 400 such visits during the year. John MacNeil's advice rings in my ears since reading his "Life" (by his wife), in which he writes from the thick of the fight on the Australian bush, back to his comrades still in an Edinburgh Divinity-school:—'As a soldier every day under fire, I have three words of counsel to send from this field of battle to recruits still on the parade-ground. The first is to *visit*, and the second is to VISIT, and the third is to VISIT, and to learn to talk to people in a ready, inoffensive way about their souls.'

I have also attended 70 meetings, chiefly women's meetings or prayer-meetings, or Taikyo Dendo meetings, held in places other than our own house. Six of these meetings have been held in the keep of the old Ainu chief of the Ainu village of Chikabumi. The Ainu understand Japanese, so I speak and pray with them in Japanese, but read the Scriptures to them in Ainu from the Romanized Batchelor translation, and teach thus simple hymns in Ainu. As far as I can see not the slightest impression so far has been produced on the men; they sit during the meeting as stolidily and impassively around the big fire-place in the hut and with as much dignity and condescension as so many great Newfoundland dogs might. But the women show feeling and interest and gratitude, and the children are as bright and responsive as heart could wish. Since we have gathered them into a day and Sunday school (January, of 1902) their progress has been astonishing.

4 *Work among the Women:*—This has taken almost entirely the "*fujinkwai*" form. In our own Presbyterian Church in Asahigawa we have a *fujinkwai* (woman's society) which last year numbered 52; of these more than half are inquirers; 31 were added during the year.

Ten of these women were brought in through our Taikyo Dendo campaign and of these seven have been baptized. We meet twice a month at each other's houses, the hostess conducting the meeting. For more than a year we have been studying the Gospel of St. John. The average number present was ten and we contributed 54 yen during the year toward Taikyo Dendo, the Dendo Kyoku of our church, church furniture and a new organ and also toward helping the poor. This meeting has been from the beginning under the superintendence of the faithful wife of our evangelist here. Once a year this *fujinkwai* sends up a delegate to Sapporo to attend the Hokkaido *Dai Fujinkwai* of which more under the head of comity.

Besides this Presbyterian *fujinkwai*, our women join once a month with the women of the Episcopal and Congregational Churches here in the meeting of the *Kyofukwai*, a regular branch of the W.W.C.T.U. This Christian Temperance Society, reports likewise to the *Dai Fujinkwai* and its annual report for 1901, its first report, (for it is only 1 year old), read at the recent Sapporo *Dai Fujinkwai*, was as follows:—

No. of pledge members (this included 7 Ainu women) 37
Average number present 21
Amount raised during the year $55.395
Objects helped: {The poor and sick, Rescue work.

A large part of the work done during the year was *rescue work*, though not losing sight of our chief object which is to *evangelize* and to *emphasize* by means of temperance methods.

The need of *Charity Relief Work, Purity in the Home and Sunday Observance*. Among the Ainu especially defined *temperance* work is sorely needed where 99% of the old men are habitual drunkards.

5 *Rescue Work:*—In a new frontier town like this, of 12000 people although only 12 years old ; and with an army post close by numbering some 8000 men, shortly to be increased to 10000; with a street nearly 4 miles long connecting town and barracks, lined with *sake* shops and their concomitant dens of iniquity on both sides of the road,— there is no form of Christian work that cries out more loudly to be done than this same rescue work. Stimulated by the accounts of Mr. Murphy's heroic work and the agitation of the Salvation Army and the Tokyo newspapers which brought on that first glorious step toward the total abolition of this horrible system,—Home Minister Saigo's famous regulation of Oct. 2nd, 1900, granting *jiyū haiyyo* (free cessation) and making punishable any attempt to restrain such liberty,— we were final stung to action by Miss Hatcher's thrilling appeal, and the Asahigawa Christian Woman's Temperance Society began work in earnest by printing on Dec. 4th in the Asahigawa and Sapporo papers a notice of proffered help to all women desiring to avail themselves of it. Since that time (if I may be allowed to extend my report to April of this year) 21 women have applied to the Society for help either personally or through their friends. Of these 21, 13 were set free and are now either at their homes or in the Hakodate Rescue Home, an institution supported by the Christians of the three different chui ches of Hakodate, most admirably housed in a new building by the sea-shore, and close under the eye of a medical missionary. One or two were married. But not all of these can truly be said to be rescued. Two left the Home, and though still in communication with it have not yet been willing to return. Two others have disappeared owing to fear and a misunderstanding of our motives. But the five now in the Home are doing good work in Japanese and foreign sewing, Japanese and foreign cooking, the use of the sewing-machine, and Chinese embroidery. One has been recently received as a catechumen. Of the 8 who are still prisoners, 3 are so against their will, but dare not brave their keeper's wrath and escape, one was unaccountably sent back by the police (who however on the whole have stood nobly by their duty and us) and 4 declined to be set free. The task of receiving the women and sheltering them for a few days, or sometimes only a few hours (for the sooner they leave this town the better) has not been nearly as trying as we anticipated, but the task of visiting the women, who either take shelter or are detained at the police-station, or in prison,

and kindly and patiently teaching and persuading them of righteousness day after day, sometimes for ten days on a stretch, has been no light one. And this work has been done faithfully and cheerfully by thirteen noble little Japanese women of our Temperance Society. When we remember the natural timidity and conservatism of Japanese women and the shrinking that any refined nature must feel among such sights and surroundings, must we not say that this is another of the "Kami no Waza" for which we thank Him and *His* Taikyo Dendo Spirit and influence.

6 The *Ainu* Work,—(there are about 400 Ainu in the scattered collection of Ainu huts lying about a mile from this town that form the Ainu village of Chikabumi) has been chiefly that of visiting and receiving visits and the holding of such simple meetings in their huts as described above. The women are more accessible than the men as to their hearts but it seems impossible to get them to attend meetings with any regularity, busy as they are from morning to night toiling in the field, and at the loom, hewing wood and drawing water for their lazy lords. The children now come regularly to a day and S. school we have started; but I am again poaching on next year's preserves as the school was only begun in January of this year. We took care to include the Ainu in our Taikyo Dendo campaign, making a lantern procession with banners and hymns, going to their village and inducing some 15 or 20 to attend our meetings one evening.

7 *Work among the Children:*—Besides the regular Sunday School work in which Mr. Rowland's Jikkai no Uta, and Miss Browns' 'Yukihira' Christmas hymns and the Tokiwa "Chaincards" and the Mitani "Fukuin Shōka" were of the greatest help, and which culminated in a *Union* S. school Christmas festival (of the three denominations) which sent a delegation out with a basket of good cheer to sing and recite Christmas dialogues to the Ainu children of the Ainu S. school at Chikabumi. An effort was made to reach the children of our Christians in a more close and personal way and this was done by organizing a Junior Endeavor Society which meets twice a month in our house with an average attendance of 20 children, who are being trained to pray and conduct meetings on C. E. principles and to keep C. E. pledges. These children took an active part in our Taikyo Dendo campaign, distributing tracts, carrying lanterns and singing hymns in the processions and contributing of their money and prayers.

One little girl of six and one boy in his school cap and uniform marched every day during our 2 weeks' campaign. Still another form of children's work that grew directly out of Taikyo Dendo was the children's meetings that were held for half an hour at church before the regular Sunday service. A short bright song service (with the Mitani hymnbook) was followed by a crisp ten-minutes gospel talk, often with questions and answers with the children, and closed by a very short prayer, after which a cordial invitation was given to attend S. school on the following Sunday and then the children promptly dismissed.

8 *Church Services.*—A special effort was made this year to vary the church services in form and character. This too was an outcome of Taikyo Dendo. I have just spoken of the *children's meeting* on Sunday evening. This was immediately followed by a *Gospel* meeting, the feature of which was (besides plenty of bright cheery hymn singing from the Mitani hymnbook, and the substitution of one or two short pointed Gospel talks for the old-time formal sermon,) that before the close, direct appeals were made to the hearers to make a decision then and there, exactly as was done in our Taikyo Dendo campaign meetings and with very satisfatory results. Such inquirers were then asked to join the weekly inquirer's class where definite instruction was given in the Bible with Pastor Okuno's small catechism used as a manual. This was held just before the regular midweek prayer meeting and so secured the attendance of the new converts on both meetings.

Toward the fall of the year a Christian Endeavor Society was organized among our church members, which meets on every Sunday evening in the church just before the service and has proved a remarkable success in the way of bringing the people out to church and stimulating their interest in Bible study. It is one of the best methods of conserving the results of Taikyo Dendo, I believe.

9 *Itinerating.*—I made 6 evangelistic trips during the year but "itinerating" is a large word for such a simple and enjoyable undertaking as a trip to Sapporo and Otaru by rail, with good foreign food and bed awaiting one an the other end, not to mention the pleasure of using one's mother-tongue with some ten on twelve other missionaries, as is the case in Sapporo. It might rather be described as plunging into the vortex of society, after the solitudes of Asahigawa. But two of my trips did take me into less alluring surroundings. One in March

which is mid-winter with us, to one of our remotest outstations, Mombetsu, 20 miles off the R. Road is still fresh in my memory. My first stop was at the part Ainu part Japanese village of Horobetsu on the bleak wreck-strewn east coast where I had the honor of attending as Mr. Pierson's representative the annual "Iburikoku Dai Shimbokkai," a very popular religious sociable gotten up by all the Christians of every denomination in that region. This year it partook of the Taikyo Dendo type of an evening preaching meeting followed on the next day by a sociable which was graced by the presence of the village authorities in full canonicals, the local daimyo, who is a faithful and earnest member of our Church, and the old Ainu chief in his embroidered elm bark coat, a living image of the old patriarchs. Everybody made a speech, the mayor, the daimyo, the old Ainu chief, and they were all good and to the point. But when a young Ainu catechist (a C. M. S. worker) sprang to his feet and made a fiery plea for his people: "You talk about your great Taikyo Dendo, but what forward movement are you planning to help *my* people! Are *they* not men? have *they* not souls to be saved?"—every eyes was riveted on him and a hush fell on the little company. He seemed like another Shylock pleading for justice and he spoke with the zeal and fire of one of the Hebrew prophets. If there are many such among they younger generation of Ainu men, there is good hope for the race. The next stage of my journey was made in an open boat crossing Volcano Bay from Mororan to Old Mororan. As we approached the little cove behind which this tiny Ainu village lies hidden a snowstorm overtook us, and the boatmen refused to go any farther and prosposed landing me on the rocks a mile this side of the village. I did not object to the rocky landing but stipulated that my luggage must be carried to the village, which after some demurring was done and the landing à la Pilgrim Fathers likewise accomplished. A half an hour's walk against a driving snow-storm brought me to the village-inn where a horse must be secured for the 8 or 10 miles of the last part of my journey. Mounted on the packsaddle of a shaggy but sure footed Hokkaido pony and with a sturdy little Ainu woman with a curious velvet headdress and a man's overcoat astride another for my guide, I was soon climbing the steep little bluff behind the village, thankful to be on terra firma again, when an ominous snap in my gear preceding a general slipping and giving way of my saddle had all but brought me into very sudden contact with terra firma. In a trice the little Ainu woman was off her horse and had sprung like a monkey on my upheaving saddle while a strong hand suddenly came to my support on the other side which proved to be no other than my young Ainu prophet of the day before making his way back on foot to his station from the meeting. After a cordial chat we galloped on with no further adventure, except the trifling one of having my Amazon guide quietly turn me over to a young Ainu man without my knowledge or consent, the exchange only being detected when, as the wearer of the velvet headgear and man's overcoat looked back to smile reassuringly at me, I saw to my surprise that the mouth no longer wore a moustache, thus betraying the fact that its owner was *not* a woman! By this time the woman had utterly disappeared, being well on her way back to her home; so there was nothing to do but to jog along behind the man and trust myself to Providence. Presently I bethought me to ask: "Do you know where I want to go in Mombetsu?" "No, he said, cheerfully but I suppose you do." "All that I know is that I want to go to be house of Kayapa." "I know where that is," he said and sure enough to the house of Kayapa and the home of our evangelist he brought me safe and sound in spite of roads over which let us a draw the veil of charity, for I am persuaded nothing else could be *drawn* over them.

The next evening our Evangelist, the Ainu C. M. S. catechist and I held a Taikyo Dendo meeting in our church which was packed and the Ainu preached with such fire and force from Mark 1,:2: "*they were astonished at his doctrine; for he taught them as one that had authority and not as the scribes,*" that one Japanese (who has since received baptism) was converted on the spot.

As I write, the following has just reached me from Mr. Pierson off on a trip in this same region. It is so characteristic, not to say Hokkaidoesque, that I can not refrain from putting it in:

I must tell you a story of a little girl and a bear. Mr. I. of Abuta, (some 6 or 7 miles beyond Mombetsu) one of our believers, has a little girl about 9 years old. When she was 7 years old, a festival was held at *Usu* (a village 2 miles off) to which her father went to sell toys; the little girl was sent from her home to take him some *O musubi* (riceballs). She took the shortcut and missed her way, going some distance out on a path towards the mountains. It was day-time. She found

127

herself suddenly, confronting a bear. She knew it was of no use to run away. She determined to be friendly. The bear growled. She bethought herself of the rice-balls slung around her shoulder: "Ojisan, ojisan, (uncle!) is this what you want?"

She reached him one. The bear came near enough to her to take it, broke it open and hesitated. "Ojisan, ojisan, you know I wouldn't fool you, there's no poison in it." So the bear ate up the rice-balls. "Why ojisan, there's a rose-bramble on you; I'll take it off for you." She even patted him and he didn't resent it. "Well, Uncle, I'll be going. Good bye;" and as she started off in the *wrong* path, the bear growled. She looked back and the bear motioned with his head in the direction of another path. "Ah! wakatta! wakatta!" (I see, I see) said she and bowed her farewell. "Good bye, Ojisan. Thank you;" and the bear seemed to bow his head too.

And the sequel, is almost as good as the story. "Why, said her father didn't you tell me this at the time." "Because I had lost my rice-balls and I was afraid of a scolding." The little girl insists that all this happend.

It is "so beautiful, it must be true," as Kingsley said, and if it isn't, the child that could invent such a tale as that, is a genius and will end up by being a Kipling or a Seton-Thompson some day.

Yesterday I came very near having a bit of "itinerating" to do right here at home. On my way to our Y.M.C.A. building at Chikabumi where I hold English Bible classes 3 times a week for the men and officers of the Army Division stationed here, I have to cross a long bridge spanning the Ishikari River. the largest river in Japan.

When I reached the bridge, it was gone; the river had risen in the night during a terrific down-pour and the great bridge had been swept a half mile down the stream. To see the largest river in Japan overflow its banks is something worth seeing. It was the color of the Mississipi but it had the rush and swirl and unearthly swiftness of the Colorado or the Kicking Horse as they go tearing through their canyons. And this river is very broad too, the current making great swelling waves. I think I never before saw what might be called "waves" in a river, certainly not at a point over 100 miles from its mouth. Attempts were being made to launch a big flat-bottomed boat, and as I was due on the other side for my lesson, I expected to cross the river on this strange craft. That would have been exciting and interesting but on looking across I discovered that where you reached dry land you apparently had to wade through a foot of water along the road for some time; I would do a good deal for my soldiers, but that did give me pause, and I was not sorry when after the boat capsized once on twice near shore, the attempt was given up. Later some Ainu men were called in to get the boat across but even under their skilful management, she capsized again in midstream By this time however a rope-ferry has been established on which I hope to cross to-morrow to attend my Ainu S. school and the soldier's preaching service.

10 *Taikyo Dendo*.—(Please see my paper on this in the Japan Evangelist for April and May, 1902.)

A Word on " Comity."

1 The *Hokkaido Dai Fujinkwai* is an interdenominational Union Woman's Conference of all the *fujinkwai* in the Hokkaido. It held its first formal meeting 8 years ago in the historic Sapporo Independent Church. It is held alternately in one of the 5 Christian churches in Sapporo, usually in the spring of the year. This year its meeting was held on the same day as the Tokyo and Yokohama Dai Fujinkwai and the Kyoto and Osaka Dai Fujinkwai to both of which it sent a telegram of greeting. This year it was attended by nearly 300 women, 245 of whom sat down to lunch together at Miss Smith's Girls' School (Presbyterian,) in Sapporo. The majority present were Presbyterians judging from the list of names handed in, thought many did not register. Thirty seven different woman's societies were represented, 10 Presbyterian, 10 Episcopal, 6 Congregational, 5 Methodist, 1 independent and 5 temperance or charity societies. Twenty-one Hokkaido towns sent reports or delegates, Sapporo furnishing however by far the largest number. The society having the largest membership was the Congregational *fujinkwai* of Sapporo with 56 members, the Otaru Episcopal and the Asashigawa Presbyterian close seconds with 52. The society which had collected the largest amount of money during the year was the Hakodate (Presbyterian) with 82 yen.

2 *The Hokkaido General Conference* for all missionaries and Japanese workers in the Hokkaido met last year for the first time in Hakodate and was a marked demonstration of *comity*, not to say *unity*. The proceedings lasted a week and were conducted entirely in Japan-

ese, except for one short English session attended only by the foreign missionaries. The Conference was attended by nearly 100 persons and at the close it unanimously voted to meet again the following year in Sapporo. (It had a very successful meeting this fall).

3 The *Ainu* work is a practical experiment in comity,—all the Ainu coming by an unwritten law under C. M. S. jurisdiction. Those in our region belong to the district in charge of the C. M. S. missionary resident in Otaru. He supplies me with books and good advice, and I do the work as his "unpaid helper." When the point of asking for baptism is reached, our Chikabumi Ainu will, I hope, enter the fold of the Sei Ko Kwai, to which all the Ainu Christians belong.

4 *Taikyo Dendo* was of course a triumph of inter-denominational comity, especially here in the Hokkaido. So saturated are our Christians with comity ideas, that when a noted Presbyterian divine from Tōkyō came up to hold meetings for Simon-pure Presbyterians only on strictly denominational lines, people simply rose as one man and demanded a union Taikyo Dendo meeting and got it too. Fortunately the man was big enough to rise to the occasion and preached a straight strong gospel sermon to about 100 people. The strictly Presbyterian meeting was attended by 17 people. Another amusing illustration occurred when the Rev. Kiyama came to tell us the story of the Daikwai Dendo Kyoku. It got abroad that he was to hold a woman's meeting in our house. The idea was to speak to our Presbyterian women only, with a view to getting them interested in the Dendo Kyoku. But when the women of the other churches heard that a noted Tokyo pastor was to hold a woman's meeting they cheerfully sent word to us that they were coming to the meeting and come they did. Sectarianism seems to die a natural death in this broad isle.

Finally, a word of counsel or warning is called for.

Four practical points greatly needing definite, special and urgent *attention*, suggest themselves:

1 The matter of *church membership registering* and *letters* of *dismissal*. Can not more system and care be brought to bear on this point ? The Hokkaido is full of home-less church members with their "*seki's*" in Osaka, or Yamaguchi, or Nagasaki or anywhere except the place at which they are residing at the present moment. Thus they are a loss to their own local churches, and a very uncertain if not a minus quantity in the churches of their new home. Moreover not being definitely

connected with the church where they now live, they attend irregularly and sooner or later their faith goes under. The Episcopalians and Methodists (I believe) have a very simple device which prevents this, that of giving the departing Christian a letter of transfer *as soon as he leaves his former locality*, and of notifying the pastor in the new locality *that the transfer has been made*. With us the transfer is left entirely to the initiative of the Christian who in 9 cases out of 10 simply takes no action at all. When I have remonstrated with any one for not asking for his *seki*, he tells me it is *okino doku* (sad, too bad) for his old pastor to whom he has "*giri*" (a duty). When I urge the new pastor to ask for it he declines on grounds of etiquette—and so all around a "state of masterly inactivity" is preserved in the course of which the Christian back-slides, the old church loses both him and his financial support, and the new church likewise fails to secure either. Among such an ever-shifting population as the Japanese, this is a vital question, affecting the prosperity of the church in every part of Japan. Can not the Council recommend some suitable course of action to the Dai Kwai and to churches?

2 *The Marriage Register.* It is unfortunate that even some *missionaries* do not appreciate the importance of the marriage *seki*. No marriage however solemnly celebrated by all the rites of church is *legal* unless the *seki* has been properly secured *beforehand*. Japanese custom prefers to arrange the *seki after* the marriage has been accomplished, *but this is not Japanese law*. Surely the Christian Church can not afford to lag behind the *law*. All that is necessary is an agreement or law that the officiating pastor shall make sure that the *seki* has been secured, before he is allowed to perform the marriage service. The Hokkaido General Conference passed a resolution of this kind last year. Can not something be done at the meeting of Council?

3 *Sunday Observance.* Can not some practical aggressive work be done on this line? Surely we can not hope for God's blessing while his laws are being so generally disregarded as this one is. The Tokyo Conference of 1900 appointed a committee on the work. Has its report been received? (The Japan Sabbath Alliance has been formally established by a general convention this fall, and plans for work are formulated).

4 *Rescue Work.* Has not the time come for us missionaries as individuals to take up this work as a most practical and vital part

of our missionary work. Until now it may have been premature, but surely this can not be said now with the *law* on the side of righteousness, and the best element among Japanese public men, like Ando Taro, and Nemoto Sho working with their might and main to break up the iniquitous system that still prevails. If we 782 missionaries in Japan and especially we 252 missionary wives rose in our might, nay, in the might of the Lord Jehovah, shall not "one of us chase a thousand" for the Lord our God. He it is that fighteth for us *as he hath promised.*"

III

APPENDIX

I

WORK OF THE BIBLE SOCIETIES COMMITTEE IN JAPAN.

To the Council of Missions Cooperating
   with the Church of Christ
      in Japan.

Dear Brethren:

    As it is usual for the Bible House to be represented at your annual conference I am writing to express regret that for this year it cannot be so. Mr. Loomis is still absent on furlough in America. Mr. Parrott, as you are all aware was summoned last month to England, to attend the death-bed of Mrs. Parrott, who passed away before he could reach home. Mr. Snyder has gone to America. And I, myself, have to be in daily attendance at the office; so that, for the first time for many years, we shall not be directly represented at your annual conference.

    Instead of the usual remarks which you have been accustomed to hear of the work going on at the Bible House, and also in the field, I beg leave, respectfully to submit to you a few general matters.

    The unfortunate fire at the Bible House in February last besides destroying almost the entire stock of Scriptures then on hand, quite disorganized the office and seriously hampered the work for many weeks. Fortunately our stock of plates which had been stored in the cellars of the Bible House was found to be uninjured, and we were therefore able to obtain fresh issues of Scriptures in a comparatively short time. But for this fact new orders for Bibles from all parts of Japan could not have been supplied for many months; and the work of missionaries, evangelists and colporteurs, would have been much hindered thereby. The Bible House has since been rebuilt and is almost finished; the fittings alone not being quite completed. We have removed there, the whole of our stock from the temporary premises at No. 82 Seamens Mission, and in another week or ten days we hope to be in full working order again.

Circulation and work in the field has likewise been hindered. First, by the limited supply of Scriptures necessary for colportage. Then when fresh issues were to hand, Mr. Snyder withdrew from the work in order to return to America, and I was called in to take Mr. Parrott's place in the office; consequently, there has been a serious shrinkage in circulation during the last three months. Looking forward to the end of the year we must expect a large diminution in circulation, nor can we anticipate anything like the splendid returns of last year which totalled over 186,000 Scriptures.

Against this, however, we have at least one cause for encouragement. One of our Japanese colporteurs, Mr. Katsumata, who has been trained for the work has met with great success during the last six months. At the great festival recently held in connection with the Tenjin Temple in Kyoto, Mr. Katasumata's sales totalled over 3500 Scriptures in less than seven weeks, and again in the Hokkaido he has circulated over 2000 copies in one month. I am glad to state that he is still maintaining this high average. These results will be better understood when I explain, that none of our other corporteurs dispose of more than 1000 Scriptures in a whole year. Thus it is easily seen that Mr. Katsumata is a valuable addition to our colportage staff; and if his success continues to the end of the year our total returns for the twelve months may not be so small as we anticipate.

I may add that Mr. Katsumata has proved himself useful in assisting some of the missionaries; but more especially, evangelists who are stationed in various towns through which he has travelled. He has taken part in many Sabbath services and has also assisted in numbers of week night meetings.

Mr. Snyder concluded his work at the end of May. He had spent most of his time since January in Kiushiu and met with unqualified success. I am not able to state the totals of his sales but they have reached high figures.

While Mr. Snyder was at work in Kiushiu I myself visited Shikoku where I journeyed to a large number of towns and villages. I am glad to say that wherever I traveled I found the people well disposed to our work. Previous to my trip to this island very little systematic colportage had been attempted; and since we have found that a good demand for the Scriptures exists there as well as in the other parts of Japan we have all the more reason to be thankful.

I regret to say that Mr. Loomis' continued ill-health will not permit him to return to Japan as soon as he had expected, but we expect him back in September.

It is also my sad duty to refer to Mr. Parrott's affliction in losing his devoted wife in England; the fact of her passing away before Mr. Parrott could reach home, must have been doubly hard for him to bear. Deepest sympathy has been expressed by numbers of his friends all over Japan. We are looking for his return in about another month.

In conclusion I am thankful to say that throughout the Empire there is still a desire among the people to possess copies of the Holy Scriptures. The spirit of inquiry seems still to be widening and deepening. The Lord's promise that His Word shall not return unto Him void, is being fulfilled in our midst; and we have many evidences that it does accomplish that whereunto He sends it. May we not then again thank God and take courage. The Bible Societies' workers earnestly desire to open up fresh fields for the devoted missionaries to follow on and labour, and to scatter the good seed of the Kingdom, broadcast over the land, for them to gather rich and bountiful harvests. May this be the happy and blessed results from the labors of us all.

      I am, Brethren,
       Yours in His service,
         A. LAWRENCE.

II
STATISTICAL TABLES.

MISSION STATISTICS FOR 1901-2

MISSION OF THE	Missionaries — Men — Married Or-dained	Unor-dained	Unmarried Or-dained	Unor-dained	Women Unmar-ried	Total Includ-ing Wives	Stations Where Missionaries Reside	Out-stations	Educational Work of the Missions Theological Schools	Students in Theo. Schools	Bible Wo-man's Sch. or Dept'n	Students in Same
Pres. Church in U.S.A.: East Japan	6	1			11	25	5	24?	¼	5	1	15
West Japan	10				12	32	7	29				
Totals	16	1			23	57	12	53	¼	5	1	15
Refd. (Dutch) Church in A.: North Japan	5	1			6	18	5	24	¼	4	1	1
South Japan	4		1		3	12	3	15	1 sus-pended		1	1
Totals	9	1	1		9	30	8	39	1¼	4	2	2
Pres. Church in U.S. (South)	10				7	25	9	70	¼	4		
Cumberland Pres. Church	4		1		7	16	6	?			1	12
Womans Union Miss. Society					3	5	1	5			1	26
Refd. (German) Church in U.S.	6	1	1	1	4	18	2	47	1	11	1	8
Totals for 1901	45	2	3	1	55	153	28	234+	3	24	6	63
Totals for 1900	47	2	2	1	49	150	27	170+	2	17		
Increase			1		6	3	1	64?	1	7		
Decrease	2											

MISSION STATISTICS FOR 1901-2—(Continued)

Educational Work of the Missions—(Continued)

MISSION OF THE	Boarding Schools for Boys	Pupils in Same	Boarding Schools for Girls	Pupils in Same	Day Schools incl. Kindergarties	Pupils in Same	Christian Pupils in all Schools	Number Professing Christianity during the Year	Foreign Teachers Men	Foreign Teachers Women
Pres. Church in U.S.A.: East Japan	4	90	2	331	6	390	152	51	2	11
West Japan			3	142	5	321	57	10		10
Totals	4	90	5	473	11	720	209	61	2	21
Refd. (Dutch) Church in A.: North Japan	1	90	1	96			82	24	2	2
South Japan	1	100	1	55			21	1	2	2
Totals	2	190	2	151			103	25	4	4
Pres. Church in U.S. (South)			1	45			40	6		2
Cumberland Pres. Church			1	50			?	?	1	1
Womans Union Miss. Society			1	63			31	15		5
Refd. (German) Church in U.S.	1	120		70			92	38	7	4
Totals for 1901	3	400	11	852	11	720	475+	149+	10	40
Totals for 1900	3	312	11	821	11	768	423+	102+	9	29
Increase		97		26			52?	47?	1	11
Decrease						48				

MISSION STATISTICS FOR 1901-2—(CONTINUED)

Mission of the	Ed. Wk.—(Con.)			Evangelistic Work of the Missions						
	Japanese Teachers		Grants from For. Miss. Bds. for Ed. Wk.	Japanese Preachers Ord. and Unord. Receiving Salaries from the Missions	Salaries of Same	Itinerating Expenses of Same	Bible Women Receiving Salaries from the Mission	Salaries of Bible Women	Itinerating Expenses of Bible Women	Granted by For. Miss. Bds. for Evangelistic Work
	Men	Women								
Pres. Church in U.S.A.: East Japan	19	20	11230	19	5364	274	11	995	91	9366
West Japan	15	31	7469	23	6766	540	8	990	116	11483
Totals	34	51	18699	42	12130	814	19	1985	207	20849
Refd. (Dutch) Church in A.: North Japan	9	8	6246	15	3366		3	263		5321
South Japan	11	15	6100	13	4710	395	2	144		5600
Totals	20	23	12346	28	8376	395	5	407		10921
Pres. Church in U.S. (South)	3	4	1750	20	4642	985	5	662		7728
Cumberland Pres. Church	4	5	1200	10	?2500	?200	7	?900		4000
Womans Union Miss. Society	5	8	4514				36	24500	530	7370
Refd. (German) Church in U.S.	22	10	13687	41	7248	1128	17	1406	234	10719
Totals for 1901	88	101	51996	141	34896	3522	89	9920	1021	61587
Totals for 1900	78	96	45224+	128	32642	4325	97	10248	1426	62713
Increase	10	5	6772	13	2254					
Decrease						801	8	328	405	126

SUMMARY BY PRESBYTERIES (AND GRAND TOTALS)

PRESBYTERIES	Membership Meiji 34 (1901) January 1st			Baptisms			INCREASE Restored			Received from other Denominations		
	M.	W.	C.	M.	W.	C.	M.	W.	C.	M.	W.	C.
Tokyo	2141	2254	650	328	197	39	11	12	1	14	10	1
Naniwa	1368	1339	510	146	126	60	5	1		15	16	
Sanyo	162	192	96	17	18	3	1	3		1	21	
Chinzei	196	202	113	22	21	8	1			5		
Miyagi	969	674	109	174	76	35	1	4		10	4	
Grand Totals 1901	4836	4661	1478	687	438	145	19	20	1	45	20	1
Grand Totals 1900		10830		329	235	114						
Increase (=+) Decrease (=—)		+45		+368	+203	+31						

139

SUMMARY BY PRESBYTERIES (AND GRAND TOTALS)—(Continued)

PRESBYTERIES	INCREASE—(Continued)								DECREASE											
	Received						Confirmations		Dismissals						Dismissed to other Denominations			Deaths		
	From Churches of other Presbyteries			From other Churches of same Presbytery					To other Churches of same Presbytery			To Churches of other Presbyteries								
	M.	W.	C.	M.	W.	C.	M.	W.	M.	W.	C.	M.	W.	C.	M.	W.	C.	M.	W.	C.
Tokyo	33	27	5	25	31	6	11	14	29	39	9	23	20	4	30	31	12	19	30	4
Naniwa	32	25	9	36	51	15	12	11	33	46	14	31	20	2	7	6	1	25	12	2
Sanyo	3	2		5	13	3	3	1	5	10	3	8	11	6	1	1		1	4	1
Chinzei	4	1		6	4	5	1	2	11	11	1	6	17	3	9	14	3	8	7	1
Miyagi	7	11	5	15	11	2	11	12	19	14	5	16	9	3	3	1	1	13	11	1
Grand Totals 1901	79	66	19	88	110	31	38	40	97	120	32	84	77	18	50	53	17	66	59	9
Grand Totals 1900							11	15										84	67	19
Increase (=+) Decrease (=—)							+27	+25										−18	−8	−10

SUMMARY BY PRESBYTERIES (AND GRAND TOTALS)—(CONTINUED)

PRESBYTERIES	DECREASE—(CON.)						Membership Meiji 31 (1900) December 31st				SPECIAL ITEMS								
	Erasures			Excommunications							Resident Elsewhere			Residence Unknown			Debarred from Communion		
	M.	W.	C.	M.	W.	C.	M.	W.	C.	Totals	M.	W.	C.	M.	W.	C.	M.	W.	
Tokyo	96	59	21	11		9	2355	2357	627	5339	684	626	125	127	102	18	14	10	
Naniwa	72	46	10	2	2	2	1431	1429	539	3399	542	394	120	6	4	4	1		
Sanyo	7	1	5	2	1		164	200	98	462	49	40	36	19	17	2	1		
Chinzei	15	3	1	1		1	215	196	114	525	85	76	33	6	6		5	1	
Miyagi	15	6	3				1093	716	117	1926	389	252	41	15	18	3	26	6	
Grand Totals 1901	205	115	40	16	13	12	5258	4898	1495	11651	1753	1577	355	173	147	27	47	17	
Grand Totals 1900	160	87	16	13	13	15	4836	4661	1478	10975	1714	1333	358	172	134	31	64	32	
Increase (=+)	+45	+28	+24	+3			+422	+237	+17	+676	+39			+1	+13				
Decrease(=—)						-3						-16	-3			-4	-17	-15	

SUMMARY BY PRESBYTERIES (AND GRAND TOTALS)—(Continued)

PRESBYTERIES	SPECIAL ITEMS (Con.)				Average Attendance on Sabbath Services		Average Attendance on Prayer Meetings		SUNDAY SCHOOL ITEMS								
	Actual Attendance on Lord's Supper		Totals						Children			Adults		Average Attendance		Teachers	
	M.	W.			M.	W.	M.	W.	Boys	Girls		M.	W.	M.	W.	M.	W.
Tokyo	1510	1607		3117	842	924	334	240	802	1064		157	167	701	992	97	91
Naniwa	908	981		1889	561	585	256	211	470	577		294	257			90	91
Sanyo	101	140		241	109	95	43	38	140	142		66	50	222	110	17	13
Chinzei	135	121		256	137	127	81	63	325	432		176	117	191	195	17	13
Miyagi	611	445		1056	466	287	196	127	1058	1124		84	65	583	642	62	45
Grand Totals 1901	3265	3294		6559	2115	2018	920	709	2801	3639		774	665	1697	1939	283	253
Grand Totals 1900									1985	2405		614	665			284	255
Increase (=+) Decrease (=—)									+816	+1234		+160	0			—1	—2

SUMMARY BY PRESBYTERIES (AND GRAND TOTALS)—(CONTINUED)

INCOME AND EXPENSES

PRESBYTERIES	Income			Expenses						Gifts from Out-side Sources (mostly from Missions)
	Offerings	Miscellaneous	Total	Salaries of Pastors and Evangelists	Evangelistic Expenses	Charities	Contributions Dendō Kyoku	Current Expenses	Occasional Expenses	
Tokyo	20065,942	150,207	20216,149	8247,166	1202,875	304,900	802,256	5555,808	6257,182	3015,870
Naniwa	9126,670	105,140	9231,810	7727,730		111,880	538,880	3442,410	2457,910	4089,860
Sanyo	1149,316	73,797	1403,113	1629,985	80,183	27,675	248,800	415,294	58,266	1592,105
Chinzei	1168,627	126,400	1295,027	2789,930	304,885	20,743	106,789	810,189	84,712	2832,335
Miyagi	4863,358	161,113	5024,471	6632,430	134,183	101,865	149,705	2494,207	1272,402	6020,437
Grand Totals 1901	36382,913	616,657	37180,570	27027,301	1722,076	567,033	1816,520	12747,908	10130,472	17550,607
Grand Totals 1900			32445,000				1336,000			
Increase (=+) Decrease (=—)			+4735,570				+460,52			

143

SUMMARY BY PRESBYTERIES (AND GRAND TOTALS)—(CONTINUED)

PRESBYTERIES	ASSETS - Value of Church Buildings Grounds and Manses	ASSETS - Endowments	No. of Preaching Places	No. of Elders	No. of Trustees	Deacons	Deaconesses	Ordained Ministers Full Members of Presbyteries	Missionaries, Advisory Members of Presbyteries	Licentiates (Lay Preachers)	Adult Baptisms and Contributions (Rec'd. on Confession)	Total Income Including Gifts	Total of Expenditures	Churches (Organized)	Preaching Places	Totals
Tokyo	43112,770	2586.749	23	16	89	51	22	43	3	33		24034.38	22370.	34	34	68
Naniwa	40618.000	3141.630	14	55	58	25	10	18	14	19		13870.53	14279.	16	32	48
Sanyo	6256.044	247.041	4	12	13	7	2	6	5	9		3244.01	2460.	6	6	12
Chinzei	5655.750	912.000	15	17	14	5	3	3	4	12		4234.16	4148.	6	9	16 [?]
Miyagi	22609.710	396.855	29	30	40	20	6	13	7	17		11194.61	10785.	8	27	35
Grand Totals 1901	118252.274	8294.275	85	281	214	103	43	83	33	90	1213	56577.69	53942.	71	108	179
Grand Totals 1900								74	33	93	590			71	113	184
Increase (=+) Decrease (=—)								+ 9	0	— 3	+623			0	—5	—5

SUMMARY OF PRINCIPAL ITEMS COMPARED WITH THOSE OF 1900

NAME OF PRESBYTERY	Total Membership	Adult Membership	Adult Additions (Baptisms and Confirmations)	Proportion of Adult Additions to Adult Membership	S. School Members (including Teachers)	Proportion of S. School Members to Adult Membership	Contributions to Home Mission Boards	Contributions to Other Objects	AVERAGES PER MEMBER				
									Contribution to Home Missions		Contribution to Other Objects	
									1900	1901	1900	1901
1 Tokyo	5339	4712	550	.117	2278	.50	802.36	20216.15	.137	.150	2.78	2.78
2 Naniwa	3399	2860	295	.103	1776	.62	538.86	9241.81	.096	.159	3.19	2.72
3 Sanyo	462	364	39	.106	443	1.22	218.80	1463.11	.171	.171	2.19	3.04
4 Chinzai	525	411	56	.146	1080	2.63	106.80	1295.03	.203	.203	4.29	2.47
5 Miyagi	1926	1809	273	.151	2738	1.51	149.70	5024.47	.087	.078	2.29	2.61
Totals	11651	10156	1213	.1194	8415	.83	1846.52	37180.57	.122	.158	2.86	3.19
Totals for previous year	10975	9497	586	.0617	6208	.65	1386.00	32445.00	For 1899 .098	For 1900 .122	For 1899 2.47	For 1900 2.86
Increase	676	659	627	.0577	2207	.18	460.52	4735.57	.024	.036	.39	.33
Decrease												

SUMMARY OF PRINCIPAL ITEMS COMPARED WITH THOSE OF 1900—(CONTINUED)

NAME OF PRESBYTERY	Full Members of Presbytery	Missionaries as Advisory Members of Presbytery	Lay Preachers	No. of Organized Churches	No. of Companies of Believers not yet fully Organized into Churches	Total of Previous Two Items	No. of Infant Baptisms	No. of Children included in Total Membership	Total of Income Including Gifts	Total of Expenditures	Ave. per Adult Member Total Income Including Gifts	Ave. per Adult Member Total Expenditures	Gifts (mainly or altogether from Mission Boards)	Average per Adult Member for Gifts
1 Tokyo	43	3	33	34	34	68	39	627	24034.38	22570.29	4.93	4.75	3015.87	1.15
2 Naniwa	18	14	19	16	32	48	60	539	13870.53	14278.76	4.66	4.99	4089.86	1.94
3 Sanyo	6	5	9	6	6	12	3	98	3244.01	2460.20	8.23	6.76	1592.19	5.19
4 Chinzei	3	4	12	7	9	16	8	114	4234.16	4147.26	10.04	10.09	2832.33	7.57
5 Miyagi	13	7	17	8	27	35	35	117	11194.61	10784.78	6.10	5.96	6020.44	3.49
Totals	83	33	90	71	108	179	145	1495	56577.69	54041.29	5.32	5.32	17550.60	2.20
Totals for previous year	74	33	93	71	113	184	114	1478						
Increase	9	0					31	17						
Decrease		0	3	0	5	5								

III

DENDO KYOKU (BOARD OF HOME MISSIONS) OF THE CHURCH OF CHRIST IN JAPAN.

(From the Synod's Minutes).

FINANCIAL ITEMS.

Receipts for 1901.

Balance of previous year	297.680
From the fields under care of Board*	861.190
„ „ five Presbyteries†	981.359
„ various societies	322.491
„ individuals	743.299
Borrowed	200.000
Total	3406.019

*Isezaki	165.000	†Tokyo	415.980	
Mito	58.780	Miyagi	113.812	
Hongo, Tokyo.	9.000	Naniwa	315.094	
Hamacho „	9.950	Chinzei	69.033	
Yotsuya „	98.090	Sanyo	67.440	
Kyoto	160.760			
Osaka	80.000			
Okayama	60.000	Total	981.259	
Hiroshima	180.000			
Kumamoto	48.000			
Shintake, Formosa	1.700			
Tainan „	20.000			
Total	861.190			

IV

PROCEEDINGS OF THE CONFERENCE

BY THE

REV. J. E. HAIL.

The Conference met at 9:30 A.M., July 28th 1902, with the Rev. W. B. McIlwaine in the chair. After a few minutes spent in devotional exercises, Rev. J. E. Hail was elected secretary.

A paper prepared by Rev. S. P. Fulton on the subject, *What the Bible teaches on the personal preparation of Christ*, was read. The following is an outline: While there is a sense in which we may say that every thing sprang spontaneously from the heart of Christ, there is yet another sense in which we may regard him as having made a preparation for the great mission on which he came to earth.

This is what we should expect from the true humanity of Jesus. Another indication of such a preparation is the fact that he so often referred to the time at which he was to do certain things. But the unswerving energy and zeal with which he pushed onward in his work, with no apparent changes of plans or methods, indicate that his preparation was complete from the beginning.

What were the essential elements of this preparation? The thirty years of silence at Nazareth were years of preparation.

(1) The law concerning children, fulfilled in his behalf by his parents; his visits to Jerusalem, giving him an "insight into the religious conditions of the people; his home life of poverty, toil, and

obedience; his baptism and finally the temptation, were all elements in the general preparation of Christ for his work.

2 The period of his active ministry presupposes constant seasons of preparation.

a This preparation was not merely of an academic nature. It included long and careful reflection on the relations between God and man. *b* It was a preparation of experience. Jesus experienced a complete knowledge of and fellowship with the Father, he possessed an intimate knowledge of man, and he was acquainted with nature. *c* He daily fellowshiped with God in prayer. Prayer was a means of encouragement and strength to him in his daily work; and also and especially at important crises, and in his life and in his times of personal temptation. *d* Another element in his preparation was his use of the Bible, which he used for defence, inspiration, and guidance. *e* Jesus moreover, used rest as a preparation for service. *f* Jesus kept in spiritual touch with God and man. This was the great preparation which he made for his work.

After the singing of a hymn a general discussion of the paper followed.

After another hymn and a prayer, a paper prepared by Rev. T. C. Winn was read on the subject *What the Bible teaches on the methods of work used by Christ*. The following is an outline:

Our purpose is to look at the methods Christ used in teaching the gospel.

(1) He used public speech, an old art; and regularly attended the meetings of the Synagogue on the Sabbath. From his example we obtain our warrant to magnify the importance of preaching. (2) Christ made frequent use of what we call touring. It has been estimated that the missionary journeys which he made in Galilee occupied at least half the time of his whole ministry. (3) He also employed the plan of individual work for individuals. In crowded gatherings, by the way-side, in lonely places, the individual found the attention of Christ fixed upon him. (4) Another method was the use of his power to heal. (5) Finally we should not fail to notice his training up followers to carry on the work of proclaiming the gospel after his departure. The twelve whom he chose shared his trials, heard his words, and saw him. For ourselves we may say that there is not so much a call for change of methods, as for growth in likeness to him.

A general discussion followed until the hour of twelve, when the Conference after singing and prayer adjourned until 2:30 P.M.

On reassembling, after devotional exercises a paper by Mrs. G. P. Pierson was read on the subject *What the Bible teaches on the personal preparation of the missionaries.* The following is an outline:

The objects of this preparation are identity with Christ; strenuousness, especially in looking for results; and being examples to believers. The preparation for such service consists in the study of the lives of the seven great foreign missionaries: Peter and John, Stephen and Philip, Barnabas, Paul, and Timothy. Such a study teaches us that it is of the first importance to be filled with the Holy Ghost. What is meant by this is something different from that filling of the Spirit which all Christians receive at the time of regeneration. There are four steps which lead to it. There must be a thirst; a definite asking; faith; and obedience. What Moody said is true, "The world needs more sermons walking around on two legs."

In the general discussion which ensured the following points were made. (1) The paper considered only one line of preparation, though it is true the most important line. (2) Before beginning their life-work missionaries need to spend a time apart in special communion with God. (3) A book entitled "The Three-fold Secret of the Holy Spirit," contains a clear statement of the doctrine of the Holy Spirit. (3) The spiritual harvest time is always at hand though we should not always expect only fruit of only one kind, such as the baptizing of converts. We cannot see all the results of our work; we must leave the results to God. (4) It is necessary to know the religious beliefs, literature, and customs of those we meet.

Following the singing of a hymn the Rev. A. D. Hail, D. D., read a paper entitled, *What does the Bible teach on leading difficulties to the missionary workers personally?* The following is an outline:

In the Bible there are no difficulties mentioned apart from the beneficent purpose and consequent plan of God in the upbuilding of that eternal society of saints which he is gathering together in and through Christ. Let us consider the value to the missionary of looking at his personal difficulties in the light of the fact that they are presented to us in the Bible as being an integral part of God's plan of accomplishing the eternal purpose of His all-embracing love. (1) This faith helps to the solution of the difficulties which attend the problem of the missionary's physical well-being. For ideal missionary work two things are essential: hard study and health. The apostles had their difficulties. The Saviour experienced the same classes of difficulties that we do, yet he never worried nor gave way to those anxieties which tend to produce nervous dyspepsia and a whole brood of bodily ailments. He knew that all the difficulties in the way had their place in the all-wise provisions of his Father's providence. Faith in the fact that difficulties have their fixed place in our Father's purpose of love, prepares for those which arise from the illusions that we meet in missionary work. The difficulties which grow out of our vanishing illusions are the very means by which God is going to get the greatest good out of us. The truth that the missionary's personal difficulties are the means which God uses for the advancement of His kingdom, helps the missionary to get his proper personal adjustment to his work and his fellow-workers. This way of coming into contact with fellow-workers along the line of the truth that by means of them in their place God is accomplishing His beneficent aims of grace, helps us to a view of what is best in them; this is finally fatal to all missionary fusses. (2) Another class of personal difficulties comes from our work as it confronts the constitution of society amongst non-Christian nations. Our difficulties in this direction also find their solution in the divine Factor's method in our work. The Bible furnishes us a faith in the divine Factor in our work which intensifies that large hearted love which is supreme. God, by leaving this love as a living principle to be applied as occasion requires in accordance with our own personal judgment under the guidance of the Holy Spirit, secures in this way the healthiest development of both the work and the worker. Just in proportion as we fall below this ideal we shall find that our greatest difficulty is *self*."

The Conference closed for the day with the doxology and prayer.

The Conference was again called to order at 9:30 A. M. with the Rev. W. E. Lampe in the chair; after the devotional exercises a paper prepared by Rev. A. Oltmans was read on the subject *What is our relation to our Japanese brethren?*

The following is an outline:

As our work develops the question of the relation of the missionary to the growing Church becomes more complex. (1) We must first consider our relations to the Church of Christ at large and also to the historic Churches who have sent us out. These relations are twofold:—*a* We are ministers of the gospel, *b* we are representatives of Churches which hold certain great truths as essential. These form the limits of our relations with the Japanese which are four-fold. (2) As fellow-workers. As such there should be no rank in the Church of Christ. Though our duties must differ, we should sympathize with one another and appreciate one another. As helpers we are a means to an end. The Japanese workers are to be here long after the missionary is gone. There are two features involved in this thought. *a* The present evangelization of Japan largely devolves upon the Japanese brethren. We are the helpers of the evangelists; they are not our helpers. *b* The future relations of the missionary. The Japanese work is permanent; the Japanese workers must increase while the foreign workers decrease. As the candle shines for others and is consumed so must the missionary do and be. (3) As teachers. What are teachers but helpers? All are teachers no matter in what line of work they may be engaged. Teachers, unobtrusive but none the less effectively so, are many who apparently are not teachers and not teaching. (4) As examples. This has reference to our personal conduct. Our unconscious and conscious influence is so powerful that we must live the Christ-life in fulness before our fellow workers.

Immediately following this paper was read one prepared by the Rev. C. Noss and entitled, *How can we be most helpful to our Japanese brethren?* The following is an outline:

The most important thing in our work is whole-hearted fellowship with our Japanese *brethren*. These brethren are all the Japanese Christians engaged in this great work. A *helper* is one who will do and say just what he is told to say and do. These men are not the hope of the Church. The spirit of independence is needed, not so much as an end in itself but as a stepping-stone to something greater. *Love* the Japanese brother. This is the secret of *helping* the Japanese brother.

(1) The chief obstacle in our way is racial prejudice, or the sense of nationality. The sense of this difficulty must be crushed out. The way to help our Japanese brother to rid himself of this racial feeling, is to rid ourselves of this feeling. A frank, open, fearless, loving manner at first may offend but in the end will win splendid friends. (2) We should speak kind words to the evangelists and suggest to the

Christians working with them that they help them so far as they can. (3) If the worker borrows money, it should be from the missionary rather than from others, but only after a frank talk with the man. (4) They should be paid enough to ensure a comfortable living, no more and no less. The question of books is difficult. A loan library is the best solution perhaps, if due regard is had to the prejudices and likes of the users. (5) They should be brought together once a year for personal discussion. (6) Finally, to sum all up in one word, *Love* is the key to this question.

In the general discussion of the papers the following points were made.

(1) Using Paul as an example, we should do more work than our evangelists. (2) The words of John the Baptist in regard to Christ should not be applied to the Japanese and ourselves. The results of such words in the past have been most deplorable. Foreigners and Japanese are *co-laborer*, neither is servant or master. (3) The young missionary, ignorant of human nature, is liable to unjust criticisms of the people among whom he works and to expect things too high. (4) We need in some way to furnish a will-power which does not readily give up before difficulties to our Japanese brethren, who, enthusiastic in beginning work, yet seem to lack in persistency. (5) Some evangelists are too free in the use of mission funds, and, unpleasant though it is, on this line also we owe a duty to our Japanese brethren. (6) The financial question and the matter of advancing money to evangelists is perplexing. It is not helpful to the brethren to lend them money. When lending money it is well to require its return in monthly installments. Entire frankness is best in the end. Getting a "go-between," in accordance with oriental customs, to carry on the negotiations in regard to money matters, either in making propositions to help or in refusing requests, has proved a good plan. To all apparently deserving requests, such as loans for Church buildings, one mission replies, "Our money is all appropriated; if we have any extra money, you may borrow the necessary funds wherever you can, and we will pay the interest thereon for a year, [or such time as may be agreed upon.]" Other missions require each missionary to handle the funds for his own evangelists and evangelistic work. (7) Even though it seems a waste of time, the time spent in *sodan* is in its effect good. (8) In regard to the meetings of the evangelists, the experience

of one was that the men liked to discuss methods of work and their relations to the missionary. The results had been disastrous. Others reported the results good. It is well for the missionary to arrange a program in advance, covering Bible study and methods of work. It is helpful to spend a week at a time in such meetings. Let the missionary and the evangelist in whose field the meeting is held arrange the program thus: In the mornings the study of one of the books of the Bible; in the afternoons homiletics and house-to-house work. The programs should be arranged with reference to the practical difficulties and questions which the evangelists meet.

After singing and prayer the Conference adjourned for the noon recess.

The Conference reassembled at 3 o'clock; and after devotional exercises a paper by the Rev. J. H. Ballagh on *Personal Experiences* was read. The following is an outline:

I will strive to follow some of the teachings of the Bible concerning the experiences of the first missionary to the Gentiles so far as corroborated by my own.

Yano Riuzan, a shaven headed Buddhist, a *Yabu-isha*, or quack doctor, who held an inferior position was selected by the Shogun's Council of State, for a language teacher for Dr. S. R. Brown. On my arrival, Nov. 11th 1861, he became my teacher. With him I undertook the translation of St. John, more to translate the Gospel into *him* than for the use of others. In the Summer of 1864 he became quite weak. I was impressed with a failure of duty and asked him if he would be willing for me to seek a blessing upon our translation. On his consenting I made my first impromptu Japanese prayer, which seemed to impress him much and which made a remarkable impression on me. One day while explaining a picture of the baptism of the Ethiopian eunuch, he suddenly said to me, "I want to be baptized. I want to be baptized because Christ commanded it." I warned him of the law against Christianity and the fact that even should he escape, his son might not. The son, being consulted, said that whatever would please his father should be done. On the first Sabbath in November his baptism took place in the presence of his wife, son and daughter. On Thanksgiving Day, 1864, was made our last visit to Father Yano. He thanked each of us for all the kindness shown and said," I have no way of rewarding you, but I am going to Jesus' side, and I will make mention to him of your name." Yano's death brought heaven a little nearer perhaps to Japan than elsewhere.

Awazu was a young man of the Samurai class who came to me to learn English. One day, discussing the Old Testament, he said to me with great feeling, "If Jesus Christ had come in the flesh sooner than he did, people would not have known who he was." I was made aware of his becoming a Christian in his Christmas and other letters, telling of the dawn of Christ's kingdom in the world and in his own soul.

When Kenkichi asked to be baptized publicly I wrote Awazu, who decided to be baptized at the same time, and assisted me in drawing up a number of questions for making the public confession instructive to others. I instructed the candidates in the different views as to the modes and subjects of baptism, and left the choice of modes to them. They chose sprinkling. On Awazu's becoming a Christian he understood the former events of his life as showing God's favorable protection.

Other illustrations of the ordaining unto eternal life might be given; as of Father Okuno's conversion, now quite an old man, when about thirty years ago. His conversion he attributed to what he observed in Dr. Hepburn's sincerity of character.

There was a man, fifty or sixty years of age, a cripple who was carried on his son's back two or three times to Mrs. Pierson's meetings; and on my coming to his place immediately desired baptism. Afterwards he was restored to soundness of body and lived for a number of years.

A soldier suffering from *beri-beri* at Hakone, hearing a sermon of mine, became a Christian. Though given up to die, he did not die; and since I have heard reports of his living a consistent Christian life in Satsuma.

A *tofuya* came to a service I had for blind men and returned once or twice through curiosity. Then he became shy of the preacher but finally became a believer, and is now quite a successful evangelist.

A man who kept a drug-store and a pawn-broker's shop, when he became a Christian, confessed that he had shown much interest in Christianity at first to keep me from feeling disappointed at not having a crowd to hear me, and to prevent me from writing about my disappointment to America.

In a postscript Mr. Ballagh gave a different line of experiences from the above, showing that no work done with an eye single to the Master's glory will fail of a reward.

In the general discussion that followed the reading of the paper, attention was called to the following facts:

(1) The large number who originally opposed Christianity but who testified that it was Mr. Ballagh's transparent honesty which won them to Christ. (2) In early years some strangers came to Nagasaki wishing to meet Dr. Verbeck. They turned out to be Wakasa-no-Kami's daughter and her nurse; these, away from all missionary influences, had been lead to Christ by Wakasa-no-Kami, and were afterwards baptized. Later the woman moved with her husband, a bitter Buddhist, to Osaka where she helped to build some of the first Congregational churches. Her husband discovering in his travels an island without religious beliefs, tried to get the Buddhists to go there, while she tried to get some Christian worker to go there, but at that time there was no one to go.

(3) Among the 600 policemen in Miyagi Ken are 20 Christians, 13 of whom have been baptized within the last two years.

(3) Since the time when the author of the paper came to Japan, the conditions of the field were marvelously altered; the edicts were removed, and the old prejudices were weakened. (4) A lady conducted a Sunday school which was finally broken up by a bad boy who came for that express purpose. On returing from a trip to America, she found this same boy, converted during her absence, conducting the Sunday school which he had broken up. (5) Twenty-three years ago the Buddhist priests in Hikata organized a boycott against Christianity, which aroused a man who in opposition got up a "Brotherly Love Society" to study Christianity. Out of this grew a church which has never received a cent from mission funds.

The Rev. Dr. Rankin having come in, the privileges of the floor were given him and he was introduced to the Conference which listened with pleasure to the kind words which he spoke.

The Rev. Dr. Ashmore, of the Baptist Mission in China, being called on, made a short address thanking the Conference, and pointing out God's hand behind the present trouble in China.

The minutes were read and corrected; and after singing and prayer the Conference adjourned.

STATEMENT REGARDING REVIEW

The following is the substance of a statement made to the Council by a member of the sub-committee* appointed by the Publications Committee to report on the subject. To a considerable degree the material of the statement was obtained in conference with a number of the ministers of the Church of Christ in Japan.

There is general agreement that a periodical of the right kind, one suited to the needs of the Church, has promise of much usefulness. The influence of such literature regularly received and read has not been duly appreciated by the Council.

Such a periodical should be primarily designed not for the general public, nor even for the general Christian public; but rather for the pastors, evangelists and Bible-women of the Church of Christ in Japan. Ordinarily it should not be distributed gratuitously; but the aim should be to get it into the hands and establish it in the regard of those for whom it is especially intended, rather than to make it financially self-supporting. A Christian periodical for the edification of those who are devoted to the service of the Church has a claim upon the Council for financial assistance, as truly as a theological school has a claim upon it for support. A periodical of the character in mind should be published at least bi-monthly, and if possible monthly. Issued less frequently than that, its influence would be occasional rather than constant.

Regarding its contents its may be said in general that each number should contain one article that may be described as theological; one or two that are exegetical or directly connected with the study of the Scriptures; one on some topic of present interest to the Church in Japan—to cite an example for to-day, the new Union Hymn book; one

---
* Messrs. Imbrie and S. P. Fulton.

on some subject of general interest in the current history of the world, especially such a one as has an evident moral bearing either individual or national; and one a translation from some foreign periodical. An important feature should be reviews of new books; but in the reviews it must ever be borne in mind that such books as are written in English or German will never be read by most of the readers of the periodical; and that what is usually needed is not so much a criticism of the work of the writers as a good readable outline of the books. To this it may be added that there is a feeling on the part of some that translations from foreign magazines and reviews are of especial value as supplementing the work of Japanese writers by enabling the readers to look at questions from other angles of view. On the other hand it must not be forgotten that a really good translation is a thing peculiarly difficult of accomplishment; unless the work is extremely well done it is almost certain to be stiff and hard to read. A good translator must understand his original perfectly, not in letter only but in spirit also; and he must at least be able to write his own language clearly and correctly. The opinion has been expressed by a number that one reason why the EXPOSITOR was never very popular with the Japanese was because it was to so large a degree made up of translations. Another lesson learned from the EXPOSITOR is that a series of articles is as a rule to be avoided; ordinarily each number of the periodical should be complete in itself.

Experience has shown in Japan as elsewhere that the chief difficulties connected with the establishment and carrying on of a periodical are three. First there is the financial difficulty. To bring a newspaper or a magazine to self-support requires time, labor and for a long time in some form or other a subsidy. If however as is contemplated the financial burden is to be borne by the Council, that difficulty need not cause anxiety. Secondly there is the difficulty of obtaining an editor; for not every man is an editor. Given the right man he must be allowed large discretionary powers; few poems have been written by committees, and it is a rare committee that will edit a magazine successfully. The foreign editor must of course have a competent Japanese assistant. In the third place, there is the difficulty of obtaining a constant supply of articles of the kind required; and it is increasingly clear in Japan as it has long been clear at home that at least to a considerable extent good articles must be paid for. The amount given depends upon the magazine and the writer. The *Taikō* pays as high as two *yen* and a half a page; the *Fukuin Shimpō* also pays for certain of its articles. It is thought that from sixty *sen* to one *yen* and a half per page should be allowed for the paid articles in the periodical proposed. Missionaries it may be assumed would write without remuneration, and in many cases Japanese also would do so; but if the principle be adopted that no articles whatever shall be paid for, the periodical will suffer accordingly.

The general opinion is that some arrangement should be made with the *Fukuin Shimpō*, under which the editor of the periodical would be freed from the responsibilities of printing, distribution, collection of subscriptions, et cetera; and under which also the periodical would have the moral support of that paper. Three plans were considered: viz. (1) That the *Fukuin Shimpō* should publish an enlarged monthly edition, a certain number of pages to be supplied by the editor of the periodical; (2) that a monthly supplement be printed, separate from the *Fukuin Shimpō* but to be circulated along with it; (3) that the periodical be issued quite distinct from the *Fukuin Shimpō*, but as stated above having its moral support and relieved by it from the strictly business matters connected with printing and circulation. The third plan is the one preferred alike by the Publications Committee and Mr. Uemura. It should be added that no idea of joint control is entertained by either party.

The question of cost is one that can not be answered with precision. The expenses connected with the publication of the *Fukuin Soshi* suggest 1200 *yen* as a approximately correct estimate for the first year. The opinion has been expressed that sales during the second or third year may be expected to amount to from 300 to 400 *yen*.

In conclusion it may be said that in the judgment of both the Publications Committee and the ministers of the Church of Christ in Japan whose council in the matter was sought, the periodical should be published by the Council itself rather than in co-operation with other bodies of missionaries.

IV

ROLL OF THE COUNCIL

EAST JAPAN MISSION OF THE PRESBYTERIAN CHURCH IN THE U.S.A. (NORTHERN)

Ballagh, Mr. J.C., 1875†	. . .(in U.S.)	Tokyo
Ballagh, Mrs. J.C., 1884	. . . . .	,,
Haworth, Rev. B.C., 1887	. . . . .	,,
Haworth, Mrs. B.C.	. . . . . .	,,
Imbrie, Rev. William, D.D.,* 1875	. . .	,,
Imbrie, Mrs. William.	. . . . . .	,,
Johnson, Rev. W.T., 1902	. . . . . .	Asahigawa
Johnson, Mrs. W.T.,	. . . . . .	,,
Landis, Rev. H.M.,* 1888	. . . . .	Tokyo
Landis, Mrs. H.M.*	. . . . . .	,,
MacNair, Rev. T.M.,* 1883	. . . . .	,,
MacNair, Mrs. T.M.,* 1880	. . . .	,,
Pierson, Rev. G.P., 1888	. . . . . .	Asahigawa
Pierson, Mrs. G.P., 1891	. . . . . .	,,
Thompson, Rev. David, D.D., 1863	. . .	Tokyo
Thompson, Mrs. David, 1873	. . . . .	,,
Alexander, Miss Emma, 1902	. . . . .	Tokyo
Ballagh, Miss A.P., 1884	. . .(in U.S.)	,,

* Present at the meeting of the Council in Karuizawa, August 1902.
† Year of arrival in Japan.

Case, Miss E.W.,* 1887	Yokohama
Gardner, Miss Sarah, 1889 . . .(in U.S.)	Tokyo
McCauley, Mrs. J.K.,* 1880	,,
Milliken, Miss Elizabeth P., 1884	Tokyo
Rose, Miss C.H., 1886	Otaru
Smith, Miss S.C., 1880	Sapporo
Wells, Miss Lilian, 1900	,,
West, Miss A.B., 1883	Tokyo
Wyckoff, Miss Helena* 1901	,,
Youngman, Miss K.M., 1873	,,

WEST JAPAN MISSION OF THE PRESBYTERIAN CHURCH IN THE U.S A. (NORTHERN)

Ayres, Rev. J.B., 1888	Yamaguchi
Ayres, Mrs. J.B.,	,,
Brokaw, Rev. H.,* 1896	Hiroshima
Brokaw, Mrs. H.*	,,
Bryan, Rev. A.V., 1882	Matsuyama
Bryan, Mrs. A.V., 1887	,,
Curtis, Rev. F.S., 1887	Kyoto
Curtis, Mrs. F.S	,,
Dunlop, Rev. J.G. 1890	Kanazawa
Dunlop, Mrs. J.G., 1894	,,
Fulton, Rev. G.W.	,,
Fulton, Mrs. G.W.	,,
Jones, Rev. W.Y.,* 1895	Fukui
Jones, Mrs. W.Y.,* 1884	,,
Murray, Rev. D.A., D.D., 1902	Yamaguchi
Winn, Rev. T.C., 1878	Osaka
Winn, Mrs. T.C.	,,
Bigelow, Miss G.S., 1886 . . .(in U.S.)	Yamaguchi
Foster, Miss A.L.A., 1902	Kanazawa
Garvin, Miss A.E., 1882. . . .(in U.S.)	Osaka
Haworth, Miss Alice, 1888	Kyoto
Kelly, Miss M.E., 1893 . . . .(in U.S.)	,,
Luther, Miss Ida R. 1898	Kanazawa
Mayo, Miss Lucy E., 1901	,,

Palmer, Miss M.M.,* 1892 . . . . . Yamaguchi
Porter, Miss F.E., 1882 . . . .(in U.S.) Kanazawa
Settlemeyer, Miss F. 1893 . . .(„ „) Kyoto
Shaw, Miss Kate, 1889 . . . .(„ „) Kanazawa
Ward, Miss Isabel Mae, 1901 . . . . . Osaka

NORTH JAPAN MISSION OF THE REFORMED (DUTCH) CHURCH IN AMERICA

Ballagh, Rev. J.H.,* 1861 . . . . . . Yokohama
Ballagh, Mrs. J.H. . . . . „
Booth, Rev. Eugene S.,* 1879. . . . . „
Booth, Mrs. Eugene S.* . . . . . . „
Harris, Rev. Howard, 1883 . . . . . Aomori
Harris, Mrs. Howard . . . . „
Miller, Rev. E. Rothesay,* 1872 . . . . Tokyo
Miller, Mrs. E. Rothesay,* 1870 . . . . „
Scudder, Rev. Frank S.,* 1897 (in U.S.) Nagano
Scudder, Mrs. Frank S.* . . („ „) „
Wyckoff, M.N., D.Sc.,* 1881 . . . . Tokyo
Wyckoff, Mrs. M.N.* . . . . „

Deyo, Miss Mary,* 1888 . . . . . . Morioka
Moulton, Miss Julia, 1891 . . . . . . Yokohama
Schenck, Mrs. J.W., 1897 . . .(in U.S.) Nagano
Thompson, Miss Anne De F., 1887 . . . Yokohama
Winn, Miss L., 1881 . . . . Morioka
Wyckoff, Miss Harriet J.,* 1898 . . . . Yokohama

SOUTH JAPAN MISSION OF THE REFORMED (DUTCH) CHURCH IN AMERICA

Myers, Rev. C.M., 1899 . . . . . . Nagasaki
Oltmans, Rev. Albert, 1886 . .(in U.S.) Saga
Oltmans, Mrs. Albert . . . .(„ „) „
Peeke, Rev. H.V.S., 1888 . . . . . . Kagoshima
Peeke, Mrs. H.V.S. 1893 . . . . . . „
Pieters, Rev. Albertus, 1891 . . . . . Kumamoto

Pieters, Mrs. Albertus	Kumamoto
Stout, Rev. Henry, D.D., 1869	Nagasaki
Couch, Miss Sara M., 1892 . . (in U S.)	Nagasaki
Lansing, Miss Harriet M., 1893	Kagoshima
Stout, Miss A.B., 1898	Nagasaki

MISSION OF THE PRESBYTERIAN CHURCH IN THE U.S. (SOUTHERN)

Buchanan, Rev. W.C., 1891	Takamatsu
Buchanan, Mrs. W.C.	,,
Buchanan, Rev. Walter McS., 1895 . . .	,,
Buchanan, Mrs. Walter McS., 1887 . . .	,,
Cumming, Rev. C.K., 1889	Gifu
Cumming, Mrs. C.K., 1892	,,
Fulton, Rev. S.P, 1888	Tokyo
Fulton, Mrs. S.P.	,,
Hope, Rev. S.R., 1892	Toyohashi
Hope, Mrs. S.R.	,,
McAlpine, Rev. R.E., 1885	Nagoya
McAlpine, Mrs. R.E.	,,
McIlwaine, Rev. W.B.,* 1889	Kochi
McIlwaine, Mrs. W.B.	,,
Moore, Rev. J.W., 1890 . . . (in U.S.)	Susaki
Moore, Mrs. J. W., 1893 . . . (,, ,,)	,,
Myers, Rev. H.W.,* 1897	Tokushima
Myers, Mrs. H.W.*	,,
Price, Rev. H.B.* 1887	Kobe
Price, Mrs. H.B., 1890	,,
Dowd, Miss Annie,* 1887	Kochi
Evans, Miss Sala,* 1893	Nagoya
Houston, Miss Ella, 1891	,,
Moore, Miss Elizabeth, 1894 . . (in U.S)	,,
Patton, Miss A.V. 1900	Tokushima
Patton, Miss Florence, 1895	,,
Sterling, Miss Charlotte E., 1887. . . .	Kochi

MISSION OF THE REFORMED (GERMAN) CHURCH IN THE U.S.

Faust, Rev. A.K.,* 1900.	Sendai
Gerhard, Mr. Paul L., 1897 . .(in U.S.)	,,
Lampe, Rev. W.E.,* 1900 .	,,
Lampe, Mrs. W.E.*	,,
Miller, Rev. H.K., 1892.	Yamagata
Miller, Mrs. H.K	,,
Moore, Rev. J.P., D.D., 1883 .	Tokyo
Moore, Mrs. J.P.	,,
Noss, Rev. C., 1895	Sendai
Noss, Mrs. C.	,,
Schneder, Rev. D.B., D.D., 1887 .	,,
Schneder, Mrs. D.B	,,
Snyder, Rev. S.S , 1894 . . . .(in U.S.)	,,
Snyder, Mrs. S.S., ...(in U.S.)	,,
Stick, Rev. J.M. 1902.	,,
Stick, Mrs. J.M.	,,
Pifer, Miss Catharine, 1901	,,
Powell, Miss Lucy M., 1900.	,,
Weidner, Miss Sadie Lea, 1900.	,,
Zurfluh, Miss Lena, 1894.	,,

MISSION OF THE CUMBERLAND PRESBYTERIAN CHURCH

Hail, Rev. A.D , D.D.,* 1878 .	Osaka
Hail, Mrs. A.D.*	,,
Hail, Rev. J.B., D.D., 1877.	Wakayama
Hail, Mrs. J.B.	,,
Hail, Rev. J.E.,* 1900	Tsu
Lathom, Rev. H.L., 1902	,,
Lathom, Mrs. H.L.,	,,
Hereford, Rev. W.F., 1902	Wakayama
Hereford, Mrs. W.F.	,,
Van Horn, Rev. G.W.,* 1888 .	Osaka
Van Horn, Mrs. G.W.*	,,

Worley, Rev. J.C., 1899. . . . . . Yamada
Worley, Mrs. J.C.. . . . . ,,

Alexander, Miss S., 1894 . . . . . . Osaka
Drennan, Mrs. A.M., 1883 . . . . . Tsu
Gardner, Miss Ella, 1893 . . . . . . Tanabe
Leavitt, Miss Julia, 1881 . . . (in U.S.) ,,
Lyons, Mrs. N.A., 1894. . . . (,, ,,) Osaka
Morgan, Miss Agnes E.,* 1889 . . . . ,,
Ranson, Miss Mary E., 1901 . . . . . ,,
Hail, Miss A.N., 1902 (Associate Member). Osaka

WOMANS UNION MISSIONARY SOCIETY

Crosby, Miss Julia N., 1871. . . . . . Yokohama
Hand, Miss Julia E., 1900 . . . . . . ,,
Loomis, Miss Clara D., 1901 . . . . . ,,
Pratt, Miss S.A., 1893 . . . . ,,
Strain, Miss Helen Knox 1900. . . . . ,,

www.ingramcontent.com/pod-product-compliance
Lightning Source LLC
Chambersburg PA
CBHW022113160426
43197CB00009B/1011